6 IX 68

James Tetreault
6 September 1968
New York City
Barnes & Noble

PHŒNIX AND TURTLE

Enti non potest addi aliquid quasi extranea natura.

ST THOMAS AQUINAS

PHŒNIX AND TURTLE

The Unity of Knowing and Being

by

THOMAS GILBY

LONGMANS, GREEN AND CO

LONDON • NEW YORK • TORONTO

LONGMANS, GREEN AND CO LTD
6 & 7 CLIFFORD STREET LONDON W I
ALSO AT MELBOURNE AND CAPE TOWN
LONGMANS, GREEN AND CO INC
55 FIFTH AVENUE NEW YORK 3
LONGMANS, GREEN AND CO
215 VICTORIA STREET TORONTO I
ORIENT LONGMANS LTD
BOMBAY CALCUTTA MADRAS

First Published . . . 1950

Printed in Great Britain
SPOTTISWOODE, BALLANTYNE & CO. LTD.
London and Colchester

To
MARY and PATRICK O'CONNOR

CONTENTS

Introduction

INTRODUCTION

THE steaming and sticky salt water was swishing backwards and forwards with the roll of the throbbing ship, the whirr of the fans was in his ears, the westering haze through the open scuttle gilded the light-green paint of the bulkheads: this was the time of ease in a bath, for soon *darken ship* would be piped, followed by *night action stations*; clammy warmth below decks, wind and water sighing past in the night; then perhaps a quiet day with the destroyers stopping at times like terriers to listen; and afterwards, though rarely a hint of the enemy fleet, the clatter of gunnery, the shriek of the Stukas, the grey-white anti-flash hoods tacky in the heat and giving the guns' crews a fleeting resemblance to Dominicans in choir, the smiling messman with his Cornish pasties and jugs of tea during the lulls, the merchantmen steaming stolidly through the splashes against the dun African shore.

From reveries of Seaton Viaduct striding across the rising mists of the Welland Valley he had been roused to an argument with one of the engineers lying in the other bath and, overalls on the hook, making ready to go on watch and inspect his damage-control party. Would praying for the safe passage of the convoy make any difference? How could we bend the wills of the higher powers to consult our convenience and comfort? The engineer for his part was going to concentrate on his valves and gauges and emergency alternatives; at least he would be impersonal if he could not be general—he agreed of course that the comprehensive meaning of human life could not be always avoided, at least as a question. Yet for the present that must wait until the return to Gibraltar. He recognized the insufficiency of merely living from day to day, meeting difficulties as they arose but postponing to-morrow's problems. Much, he supposed, might be known about machinery by himself or about animal psychology by the other, yet both, he reckoned, might be pretty ignorant concerning the things that really matter. And so in the relaxation before danger their dialogue began.

All very well to enter minutely into the technicalities of science, but not if it meant losing all sense of general direction. But is there a universal operation order, an enduring and fundamental philosophy, perennial and wider than a provincial episode, ascertainable without much scholarship about its history? We are not ambitious and would not ask for the final revelation, the disclosure of the last mystery; enough to have some clue to the scheme that controls our comings and goings, much as the arithmetical tables govern our financial transactions. Are they still valid, the ideas we have inherited from Judaea, Greece, and Rome; the assumptions of the men who built Salisbury Cathedral and the Royal Crescent at Bath, who flocked to the *Globe* and improved the breeds of English sheep, who marched with Marlborough from the Meuse to the Danube, and who blockaded the French in Brest through months of winters' gales? Can they be put in words for their descendants who still fight in every country except their own?

This book was begun that very same night.

It is a roundabout discussion, not a plain and straightforward exposition, for the foundations of a realist philosophy are not to be exposed in a succession of diagrams. The plan is not palladian, the measure not mathematical. The argument cannot be stated in a succession of theorems; the advance cannot proceed in a straight line or be built out in a progression of cubes, but is constantly curving back to where it started from.

> The way ascends not straight, but imitates
> The subtle folding of a winter's snake.

Then again, despite the abstraction from imagery demanded by high philosophy, no other science calls for so many circumlocutions in considering its first conditions or is so dependent on motions of sympathy. It is proposed to draw on our fellow-feelings with everything human, rather than to exact a formal analysis. The problem of knowledge is taken in its most general terms, and not in such splinters as the reliability of the senses or the different stages of the concept.

The reasoning reason proves a brittle instrument when used by itself. If these pages bear to the scientific criticism of cognition the relationship of journalism to literature, that is because

the writer can find no other way of reporting the present and unpretentious humanity of his subject. A messy flood is a risk to
be run in thawing out the first principles of thought. His theme
is not original, but meditated from texts of St Thomas. Other
works have not been consulted, yet the argument is full of
memories of the teaching and writings of Noël, Maritain, and
Roland-Gosselin. Their influence is here acknowledged.

CHAPTER I

THE METAPHYSICAL MOOD

ONE purpose of a classical education is to instil a philosophical temper by fostering firm yet gentle judgements on wide issues. Such a discipline, calculated to produce a habit of mind rather than a stock of grammatical and antiquarian information, finds premature specialization and technical education in a multitude of unrelated subjects a handicap rather than a help; as Heraclitus observes, rather drily, 'the learning of many things does not teach understanding.' We do not find that a balanced judgement is bound up with book learning. Close attention to select details and complicated techniques required by the scientific curriculum have fascinated the mind into a maze. We may see the first turning ahead, but the lord knows what we are doing and where we are going. An exquisite appreciation of our immediate surroundings may be cultivated, but how petty and provisional they are. One ominous universal remains, and that is death; suddenly become more sweeping and hostile because of our pile of apparatus. 'Depend upon it, Sir,' said Dr Johnson, 'when a man knows he is to be hanged in a fortnight, it concentrates his mind wonderfully.'

It has been recommended that we should cut our way out, hacking and lopping with the sharp edge of metaphysical abstraction. 'If thy right eye offend thee, pluck it out': and as the luxury of the Delta drove men to the desert in the name of salvation so may we be forced to scrap our technical gear in the name of sanity, our second-hand clobbery for the sake of the barest minimum, our muzzy luxuries in order to keep the necessities. Before concluding to such counsels of dispassionate despair, we might do well to weigh the advantages of effecting a temporary retreat and surveying the scene apart from the medley of parts.

We are no wiser probably than our ancestors were. If theirs was a bundle of fictions, ours is a set of abuses. We certainly seem less at home in the world. True, theirs was a less problematic world, if more uncomfortable; they were more secure in their judgements about what was to happen at the end of it all; their plans could be simpler, for they lacked the instruments that clutter our path; their confidence was greater, for their erudition was less. Does some of their law still remain and does it still apply? We cannot be so complacent with the contemporary scene as to wince under the taunt of seeming old-fashioned, though we may confess we cannot, even if we would, throw off what we are and go back to the past just as it was.

But perhaps we may be able to recover the substance without harking back to the customs of a bygone age—an age that was swept away when the illuminated manuscripts went flying like butterflies about the streets of Malmesbury. We cannot be in-different to the developments and even the sophistications of modern knowledge, but we may have to be less dependent on many of its techniques. Perhaps there is a perennial and perma-nent philosophy that can shape and quicken our thoughts without recourse to the passing and esoteric conclusions of highly special-ized research; a doctrine able to start from the perceptions of ordinary level-headed commonsense as well as from the refined and intricate data presented, and sometimes constructed, by delicate and ingenious artifice.

Scientists after all began as medicine-men. Even now the use of the most elaborate instrument known to any laboratory is based at bottom on elementary sensation; despite all the scientific processing, the investigators and co-ordinators must begin from knowledge the same in kind as that enjoyed by a reflective farm-labourer; their rationality is no more cautious and vigorous, and probably far less diversified. Pain and joy accost everybody in the same language, and always have; there are constant and recurring meanings in all thinking notwithstanding the variety of the cir-cumstances. All are made from the same stuff and we cannot rid ourselves of it; neither sham nor shame should keep us from the nature in which we are born and move. The same document is there for all to read: 'Nature,' says Sir Thomas Browne, 'that universal and publick Manuscript, that lies expans'd unto the Eyes of all,' and if from meditation on the common run of ex-perience ordinary men can begin to discern meanings that are true without much qualification, no need will appear to be committed to any one culture, no call be sounded to go gothic or georgian or brave new world. Instead we might begin to trace the lines of a chart that must needs be continually checked and revised, but never torn up.

1. *A General Chart*

Few are trained to track the processes and conclusions of a specialist, though more can catch the drift of what he is about. In some cases he himself will confess that he understands his arguments only during certain periods of his professional thinking, which he conducts for the most part in the obscurity and repetitions of a routine where his computations are automatically guarded and qualified, most of which are responses to paper stimuli. Otherwise he lives with the rest of us in the commonplace sensuous medium. Unless we are careful the split is now opening out, that schizoid weakness of modern life and thought, when the large and generous convictions are non-rational and scientific conclusions are pared to points too fine for flesh and blood to feel.

To close the gap the need for religion is urged; not seldom a vague and ineffectual uplift is preached instead. The more immediate need is to set out the general background of a philosophy into which a reasonable religion can be fitted. It should be neither a piece of special research nor a sublime inspiration, neither clever nor particularly awestruck; just a settled habit of getting the general hang of things, austere perhaps in its temper but not academic in its manners, arduous but not tortuous, aware of our lowliness but not over-respectful, for the world is not too large for us to manage. It will be a metaphysics, that is a science beyond the physics. If its claim to be about the nature of things as they are can be sustained, then well and good; but something at least will be gained if it turns out to be merely a method for getting our thoughts shipshape, or for behaving with good temper in despair. From the start the enquiry should be prepared, though not content, to have its questions unanswered.

There seems no other way. The particular and experimental sciences have enjoyed a long enough run on their own and we can afford to turn our attention from them for a time. They are neither self-critical nor self-controlling: legal reform does not come from the lawyers who are more interested in what the courts of law will do than in what the law is for, nor have the mathematicians any proper theory to offer on the existence of quantity; both take their postulates from elsewhere. Historically they began when men had the leisure to be curious about the functions they were already performing and their biological adaptations to environment. Their success in heaping measurement on measurement and afterwards rationalizing their constructions and then using them to produce new instruments of discovery and production may lead us to forget that theoretic validity reposes on a more general science, just as beneficial application depends on good will. On this head the immense exploitation of the deposits and energies in the material world has not been matched by humane usefulness. The internal combustion engine has not proved an unmixed blessing. Art has been served rather than prudence, moreover the arts have been mechanical rather than liberal, and in consequence whole regions of Europe have been devastated, and not only by explosives. Look at the buildings, listen to the music, taste the food. Whatever the fault and despite the gain, the engines have run wild, even out of the control of personal wickedness; we have yet to learn how to drive them so that lives are more human, not less; how to treat them all as though they were Hoovers.

The attempt, then, to look beyond our noses should need no apology. On the contrary, it is scientism and technical research that must make excuses for not exposing a general theory, and for having operated like open-cast mining with little thought for what has been ravaged. Let us therefore enter into philosophy, though it seems strange at first and our manners not at home. Philosophy is the love of wisdom, the affection for ultimate meanings rather than the expert manipulation of details. The meanings are as ultimate as we can take them, and if at the end we may be fetched up short against a mystery, it is lazy to call mystery too soon, and unwise to despise a clue because it is not a full explanation.

'I love to lose myself in a mystery, to pursue my reason to an *O altitudo*,' said Sir Thomas Browne, but he did pursue. We may well find general reasonable patterns beyond the sciences. We should try to push back the boundaries and to enlarge the rational clearing we make in the jungle of the world, to make a place to live in, with better order and air and freedom. Perhaps after all the surrounding forests of obscurity that look so impenetrable are not so threatening and gloomy as we fear. Mysterious indeed, but welcoming. Why should they be strange when our own strangeness within ourselves, not the accustomed features of our surface, is really our deep joy and ease? Happiness wells up from the mysterious centre; what is laid on from without is merely a good time. The source lies high in the hills or deep underground, a reassurance forgotten when we have but to turn a tap to get our water.

Being and belonging, how close they are. If we can find being, we shall be kin to everything and no longer estranged. Come welcome churchyard-worms, or crabs to pick my bones, come at your appointed time, better to be food for you than lie an embalmed and antiseptic corpse—when a man can think like that, without despair and in no grudging spirit, then his metaphysics has left his skull and he is living his thought and thinking no strange and hostile world. A happy man does not fear death. But we must begin in a more cerebral way, content at first to trace the contours in a rough clearing and sketch an outline in which the particular sciences may be set.

The enterprise is to surpass our physical experiences and their immediate rationalization while yet remaining, if we can, strictly rational; to approach what is enduringly and impersonally true. Already perhaps we may have caught a glimpse of these last edges of reason, distant like the snow ridging the Sierra Nevada high above the haze of the Andalusian coast. We resolve not to be distracted by lesser truths, whatever their promise of interest and excitement. Away then they go! the subjective and personal moods, the snatches of biography, the curious pieces of literary allusion, the involved and technical experimentation, the exegesis of texts, the flashes of intuition, the lyrics of mystery, the hints of vogue. Out they go!—but easier said than done, for banished as significant forms they fly back as examples. Metaphysicians set out on a very human adventure and should expect an alternation of pride and fall: the more ambitious the climb the greater the need for images to hang on to. Such comforts of sense are not the most refined, if we are to go by the example of mystical writers in their higher ascents. In fact St Thomas is suspicious of rhetorical sublimity here, and defends his preference for an earthlier style.

Truths less than metaphysical have been hinted at, yet in fact some of them may be higher, harbingers of more personal intimacy and more complete assurance—'a dayspring to the dimness of us'. Rationalism should be careful of the temper that takes scandal at strangeness and is fastidious with squalor; the beggar that was cursed may be the Caliph in disguise. The things adumbrated in the myths may be stronger than the intelligibilities signified by rational forms. Yet so long as our course keeps to the common way of science, truths can be classified according to higher and lower; so long as conversation is with the sober and communicable characters of thought and not with the high fantastics, such comparisons can be made. There need be no appeal to awe in the making of sense.

Not that metaphysics should be expected to be so stark as mathematics, for its bareness is of a different kind. Though its abstractions are more extreme its certitudes are not so pointed, for it is not engaged directly with clear edges, with quantities and their consequent figurations and relations. If not poetic, neither is its temper euclidean. Though sensibility and movement are avoided, that is only for a period; for they can never be permanently excluded from metaphysics, which, somehow, must relish everything that is in any sense real. It draws its life from a concrete experience. It is poised with an abstraction, yet only temporarily. Its refusals are no more than the gestures of interim ethics.

We shall shun as far as possible the exactness that may be purchased at the expense of this richness. Real substances cannot be neatly fitted into an arrangement of counters. A scholastic can so easily catalogue the world as a Victorian tourist judging Calabrian customs by the maxims of Manchester. Yet to begin with schemes and clear divisions is a temptation. They prove more useful in working for an examination than in pursuing an entrancing but baffling truth. They are allowable as shorthand, but not as objects of contemplation. For those who would take them more seriously there are the scholastic manuals, which this is not.

Let us throw off solemnity, for we are having a fling. Not for us the pompous hush preceding the entrance of the master, the grand metaphysical drone, the sightless eyes of the busts, the bearded lions in fading yellow photographs. Not even for us the approved authors, still less the arid little word-spinners, the nervous and suspicious ones who pounce on anything that does not conform to their book of words, least of all the shrill ones, who are like Dr Johnson's Uncle Harrison, 'drunk every night, but drunk with little drink, very peevish, very proud, very ostentatious, but, luckily, not rich.' The subject is too serious for that mummery, that fearfulness and self-importance; too much elbow room is granted for us to need that kind of carefulness and constriction. The tang of romantic latinity was one of the medieval contributions to philosophy, another was the cockney spirit. The schoolmen were logic addicts, but they knew when to lay off. The terms of philosophy are not to be wrapped up as though they were sacred relics, duly attested by legal authority; they are to be bandied about, and better slangily than not at all. A dialectic of imagination and sympathy has to be applied before existents disclose their lively meaning. Even a metaphysical abstract is not, like Mahomet's coffin, suspended in mid-air.

Over with the wheel and then back again, the confident helmsman is not gingerly but free with now more now less, and the ship steadies on her course. So it is with the truths of philosophy, they are not exact quantities to be measured to a hairsbreadth, but central meanings resolving themselves in a swirl of analogies, moving amid situations that repeat themselves no more than do the waves. The track you may register on a chart, but not the fighting purpose in the ship.

2. Prejudices For and Against

Since we are set on inducing an appropriate mood, some of the prejudices for and against metaphysics may be dwelt on; we call them so, not because they are unwarranted, but because they express states of mind antecedent to the philosophical effort: some perhaps may have to be dismissed, but others should be taken along and included in the final reckoning. Like other evolved perfections, married friendship, the whig spirit, and man's own body, metaphysics need not disavow its origins and occasions.

Rallying the main tradition of classical thought is the summons to order and the defence of the West, the call to salvage what remains of past European greatness, especially the customs of those parts most affected by Roman rule. For a period predominantly an *action française* against forces from east of the Rhine, the movement has widened and enters combatively into the field of philosophy. There are several schools; one is a counter-reformation to the doctrine of justification by sentiment alone; another the counter-revolution to the dialectic of appetite and evolution; another the insistence on property as the counter to slavery; a fourth the cult of symmetry. Its scene was once a countryside of vine and olive, its façades were warmed by the sun, its cadences were those of Greek and Latin verse. It lends itself now to the defenders of organized religion when they would show a reason for their existence; its social philosophy, while still attracting those who travel first-class on the railways, is increasingly adopted by post-communists and others who would rebuild the unity of Europe under a reasonable law without nostalgia for the good old days.

Despite differences of style, there is a parallel movement among scientists to establish a general commentary running through all departments, a synoptic science that might serve as a system of reference in which the findings of the special sciences may be co-ordinated and the moral philosophy of scientific humanism be contained. The time may yet come when a higher institute of technology will support a faculty of literature. Civilization needs a common grammar and code if the enormous mechanisms that threaten to destroy it are to be controlled. Scientists are not devoid of respect for the humanities when they address themselves to the need, and their feeling for a contemplative calm, as against the bustle of the go-getter, may be reckoned as a prejudice in favour of metaphysics.

That the traditional contemplative philosophy should be recommended as both a social need and a serviceable system of reference for laboratory work is all to the good. Every support is needed for the fabric of culture, every aid to compose the babel of thought. But if merely a universal language or a convenience is expected, we shall find that we have more than we bargained for. Goldsmith's lines about Burke may be applied:

for a drudge, disobedient;
And too fond of the right, to pursue the expedient.

Metaphysics has its own independence, and wears the buff-and-blue of men lazily but effectively contemptuous of paternalist policies. To propose it on pragmatic grounds might prove to be like Napoleon's re-establishment of Christianity in France, dictated by the claims of public security, not by the gospel. Scientific tidiness is for wisdom, not contrariwise, and once ultimate principles are seriously brought into play metaphysics will emerge more as a guiding rule than as a useful check.

Yet how excusable is the resentment felt against claims that have passed for metaphysical; how just the scorn for the lofty patronage displayed by those philosophers who are like intellectual rentiers, men who have the leisure to indulge their private fads without the responsibility of bringing them into public service; how well-founded the conviction that the real work on knowledge is shared between the scientists and the poets. The metaphysician should be like the preacher of an established religion; all the better if he be distrustful of privilege and security; sensitive to the charge of being a windbag; nettled by Macaulay's comment on *The Prelude*—'the old flimsy philosophy . . . the old crazy metaphysics; the endless wilderness of dull, flat, prosaic twaddle'; aware of the gaps between his language and his thought, his thoughts and his subject; recognizing his falls from the sublime to the ridiculous.

The prejudices against metaphysics may be put under the headings of the scientific, the lyrical, and the diffident—the latter being the strongest. Let us take them in that order; first, to see whether the sciences make self-supporting systems; next, to see whether metaphysics is hostile to movement; finally, to ask whether it is so very pretentious after all.

3. Behind the Sciences

Patient observation and calculation and prolonged application of well-wrought techniques have built installations too vast for one mind to oversee or for the collective intelligence of an industrialized community to control. A dominion has been developed that would devour every human interest, though not now so confidently as heretofore, for the machine is now threatening to destroy itself.

A growing insecurity of theory accompanies the breakdown in practice. Once it was seriously thought that outside the economically productive machine there was nothing except the private conscience, and that had to be kept pretty secret. Body was to be untroubled by soul. What our ancestors took for echoes and reflections from another world were but the noise and glowing exhaust of the engine. The gods themselves were but the memories of primitive terrors from which science had delivered us; a science wide enough to cover the political ideology of a sub-continent, but leaving off where the Old Testament worship of some Tennessee township begins.

Our present interest, however, is in the attempt to denude scientific assumptions of any metaphysical meaning. 'O Plato,' cried Antisthenes, 'I see a horse, but I do not see horsiness.' A science tries to make itself self-sufficient, yet is constantly being pushed back beyond its data, as when the science of positive law is resolved into politics, and politics under protest is taken back to morals. For all the successes of the past and ambitions for the future, a purely observational method reaches facts always from other facts, or, more accurately, there is always another object hiding behind the object selected as the first event. Left at that, scientific research would resemble opening Chinese boxes. The mind has to break out of the particular series. And so a particular science, though analysing its own proper relationships and permitting confident sweeps in its own medium, has never criticized its own postulates, still less the ambient medium of thought and intelligibility itself, and never can. The problem of knowledge is left unanswered, and despite the ingeniousness of its processes, the conduct of a science reposes on an initial response to data as spontaneous and confiding as that of a child. The mechanics of a situation may be obvious, yet the causes remain obscure.

The elaborations may be sophisticated, but the start is naive; the top is wide, but the base is narrow; the laws are large, but not truly universal. Unanswered in every transaction lurks the query whether knowledge itself has any validity. Metaphysics begins as soon as the question is posed, even though the answer given may be anti-metaphysical. A man who says that *being* is merely a word, and that everything is just matter in motion, has gone beyond the physics. Positivism itself is a metaphysical attitude, and its stoutest adherent a metaphysician despite himself, though perhaps a bad one. He may rejoin that he really does not understand certain questions and therefore cannot be expected to answer them, but his very remark makes use of metaphysical categories, and though he may avoid the title of metaphysician, he is no freer from the imputation than the Merovingian king was from crime whose memory was praised by chroniclers because he had committed only one or two murders.

Until the questions raised by metaphysics are met, the theoretic constructions of science are like an inverted pyramid, more or less irregular according to the inner coherence of the theory, but lurching unsteadily on its point, which point is hidden by vapour. This is to look at it from outside; penetrate inside and the proper parts will be found to be clumsily finished and roughly patched together, and confessedly so, for many of the measurements are merely approximate. The passion for facts proclaimed in the palmy days of positivism has now in many cases to be content with events defined more or less as objects for which a word can be found: instead of a hearty sense of physical reality we are sometimes offered the spectacle of a shrunken nervosity fiddling with symbolic terms isolated from what they may symbolize. Yet statements still remain suffused with meanings that are not immediately suggested by the evidence in front of us, and a metaphysic is still unconsciously invoked even while its relevance is explicitly denied. But there is a give and take; a general philosophy is all the better for constant criticism from positivists. Otherwise it will be large but empty, whereas it should be tight and packed with individual experience, laced with passion and pointed to events in time; disinclined to accept the dilemma entertained by W. G. Ward: 'shall I deny the fact, or defend the principle?' It should go all the way with the facts and then make a step beyond, for one of its functions is to return again to the facts and in a later summing up endow them with a dignity positivism cannot provide.

The advance proceeds in an ascending spiral: the abstraction of metaphysics is not a final achievement remaining where it stands, forgetful of the sensibility and numbers from which it has come; nor, as Kant declared, does it perpetually revolve round the same point without any advance, but circles back from whence it came yet ever bearing upward with nothing denied. 'Most pretty and pathetical!'—to a thinker in a realist temper facts are dearer than statisticians might suspect; they are things, not incidents to distract the mind from its home with meanings; they are form-bearers, not just transient excitements.

'I wish,' said Coleridge, 'to take from history its accidentality,' and a metaphysician in his solemn way is inveterately committed to things as they are; this may condone his stubbornness in cling-ing to obsolete facts, where a working scientist is always ready, or should be so, to vary his technique and to discard one set of findings and laws for another. The latter's modes are rarely final, nor are his facts; but what he is always doing is to apply certain constant sequences and patterns lying beyond the physical evidence in hopes of finding a more imaginable scheme.

A pure scientist seeks, not the thing, but the scheme to fit it in; he is quite ruthless in his search for neatness and efficiency; he will scrap anything to suit his own convenience, and will not scruple to act as though he kicks the ladders away up which he has climbed. In the progress of physical science the images of common sense were displaced by mechanical methods, and these in their turn were displaced by mathematical calculations referring to events so qualified by symbols as to be unintelligible save to a few experts.

Lawyers can be embarrassed with the philosophy of law, and it will not be as lawyers precisely that they will discriminate between some atrocious dictate and a prudent and kindly regula-tion. Indeed self-criticism should not be expected of any particular science. You have to stand away from a thing in order to size it up, like a good tennis player lying back almost nonchalantly from a cannon-ball service. Particular methods of measurement and calculation should sometimes be laid aside in order to consider what is implied in any attempt to render a scientific account of the world. We are then left with the underlying conditions of all knowledge, to the self and its objects, to reasons that are prior to scientific facts.

We shall hope to show that these objects are not purely mental figures, but subjects of existence; but whatever the conclusion, it is important to foresee that the enquiry is bound to push into the country beyond the last clearing. We have to go there even if we may return disappointed and saying that nothing of value is there, like the men who first stumbled back from the interior of Africa. But we should be prepared to return there if we would still continue our search for explanations, not content with the settlements on the coast and along the rivers and roads.

What could be antecedent to scientific fact: what is reality in the raw? For the moment, and without prejudice, let it be called *being*. We might refer to it as *x*—the unknown quantity, or rather, the unknown before quantity, for even quantity is imagined as extending something. We can enquire, though the question makes little sense to a man who has schooled himself to restricted linguistic problems, what is this unknown, of which we may say that some aspect is measurable or numerable or somehow describable? *Being* is a better term than *x*, more traditional and in its way more modest; it is but the participle of *is* and that to begin with is a more diffident word than *has* and vaguer than any letter of the alphabet.

Is *being* then a thin concept, and in writing it up shall we be serving an austerity diet? We shall see later what nourishment may be there, but for the present it is enough to agree that the notion of being pervades every fact and every thought. The sting of incident may appear to be lacking in such an amorphous undifferentiation; yet nothing can be humanly conceived except as a manifestation of being. If an empiricist urges a metaphysician to come down to brass tacks, the latter should be prepared to rejoin sincerely that such is precisely what he is trying to do. On reflection are we not rationally more certain of being in general than of any one thing in particular, of an abstraction rather than of a concrete occurrent? The answer demands no affectation of false grandeur, no high and mighty rumbling. In origin metaphysics is a very human affair, humble and unpretentious, yet strong, like the Rule of St Benedict, for those who seek the life of perfection.

It will not be put off by a parade of complications. It stands like
the ordinary man, silenced but not satisfied by the chatter of
experts, respectful before the pundit, but still saying, 'I don't see
why . . .'

4. The Bloodless Dance

The poetical prejudice against metaphysics may be grouped
with the mathematical. Each too easily tolerates the fracture
between reason and fancy, thought and sensation. The mind is
dislocated when scientific knowledge is turned over to mathematics and all the other human ways of knowledge worthy of
respect are shifted to art. Science and letters becomes science or
letters.

Once upon a time the pythagoreans believed in the magic of
numbers, later the spirit of geometry dominated the schools and
even constructed the eighteenth-century Temple of Taste; afterwards a delineation of figures displaced the radiance of forms;
and now, left with symbolic patterns on a gridded screen, some
are returning to the mathematical mysticism of the ancients.
Yet before this sets in, we may pause at the period when philosophy had acquired a hard glitter, and was ceasing to be itself.
Advancing with an elaboration of theorems, it claimed to be an
exact science in the sense that a commercial transaction can be
termed exact; clear ideas were proferred from its meditations,
and clear conclusions refracted. For already mathematical had
become the highest epithet of praise to give to certainty—perhaps
because the most authentic translations of bodily things are, as St
Thomas notes, into figures rather than into colours. In the same
sense we speak of a dead certainty. Philosophy accepted the convention and presently became a kind of superior ornament to
mathematics.

In this delusive exactness where was sensibility and where was
movement? Where the music that is the dialectic of mathematics?
All these remained in life, but they had been extruded from the
scientific field or translated out of recognition. But must sensibility be left to romantic feeling, music to art and movement to
history? Cannot the world of quality and alteration remain a
proper study for philosophy? Precision and punctuality will of
course always distrust rhetoric—Flaming Fountains and Weeping

Fires—in the high places of the mind and try to replace shimmering identities with rock-edged ratios. But perhaps the philosopher has been too touchy to the charge of pseudo-science. He has avoided the slopes that belong to him, and has agreed not to understand what cannot be measured. On the contrary the interests of natural scientist and philosopher alike respond to sensible and moving things, and though their delineation in a mathematical scheme is legitimate and useful, the entire scientific story is not thereby provided. We look for things, not merely for a written voucher. A philosopher should be a naturalist who is a field-worker, a draughtsman who is a *plein-airiste*.

St Thomas, and Aristotle before him, speak of *acribology*, and were aware of the danger of demanding exactness in material that will not tolerate it. As if you can apportion love except in the childish game of How Much?—as much as x? more than y? A clear style may go with wit, but humour seems to require a mistier climate, and philosophy, for all its certitude, should always show a trace of cloud. It is the science of creatures, and at its best of living creatures, shadowing and lighting their inner comedy and tragedy, knowing their drawbacks, touched with surprise and pity, never completely in control as the mathematician is with his arrangement of figures.

A purely quantitive method, if only because of its edges, must exclude something; lines are drawn, real and imaginary, and there is always a frontier, though perhaps an expanding one. But always strange figures rove outside, and inside there is queerness enough once you stop thinking in the usual way. There is an impulse to a rational science in which everything is subsumed, to find wisdom even in waywardness—'sweet and sour, adazzle and dim.' Though the meditations of metaphysicians may appear to have been about the vaguest and most general meanings, yet their gesture is to everything and their deference to nothing less than to being in each and every manifestation, sublime or earthy, ambitious and humble. Would that we could adapt to a metaphysician what Horace Walpole said of Fox: that he holds his levée in Cynic weeds but with Epicurean good-humour.

Though the most fanatical metaphysicians have strangely commanded an excellent style, the ancient feud between the intellectuals and poets persist—sometimes as a false contrast when the wrong people are termed intellectuals and the wrong people poets. The muses of philosophy sang with Boethius in the darkness of his condemned cell against the muses of poetry: 'Begone, Sirens, seductive to destruction, leave him to mine to be cared for and comforted.' But whatever the reason may be, the impatience with philosophizing is not confined to people who are content to live 'a youth of frolics, an old age of cards.' After all a philosopher so easily grows a bore, like a man who can 'walk miles on the most varying April day, and never see the beautiful dallying of earth and heaven.' And when he is silly into the bargain he is the harder to bear with, because he extemporizes from solemnity, not from high spirits. Any attempt to break the tedium is welcome, even if the result of a philosophy of élan may recall the lines:

> Agamemnon grieved above the rest,
> Superior sorrows swell'd his royal breast.

The abstract analysis of the transcendental properties and implications of being have to be quickened by the myths behind the history of the individual and the race. The Ideas should be focused with the Images; the Pastoral Epistles with the Apocalypse; and the arts of literature should join the sciences, if not in their lower reaches, then at their highest spring, whence philosophy should descend. Its truth should be passionately apprehended and imaginatively expounded, and the effect should be of oratory, and perhaps of song. The aspiration of the philosopher is to know the maker and the making; to feel the pulse of being and suffer the passio entis; to know, not with the brain alone, but through every cell.

His direction, however, is all his own. Reversing the psychological impact of human perception, he starts from the far side of human experience, from what is common, not from what is peculiar. His effort is to find the first most general meaning, and he is prepared at the start to sacrifice penetration for range. He is not set on repeating or heightening a moment, nor on creating a literature or building a culture. He is not even engaged on literary criticism, he is merely the post-physicist who still remains a scientist, a man, like Socrates, able to drink deep without being any the worse, and all the better if humorous about his limitations; he will not be led to antagonize the men of sentiment, whom presently he will need as his best friends.

5. *Common or Garden*

Lastly the prejudice of humility operates against the ambition to build a general philosophy. To a proper diffidence, and certainly to intellectual timidity, the manners of some of the metaphysicians seem rather uninviting. They act like the critics of Keats, or like Rousseau loving mankind in general and hating men in particular. Furthermore philosophy is up against an instinctive reticence and dislike for pushing thinking to its utmost conclusions, indeed for having much to do with extremes.

> Women make men love, and love makes them sad;
> Sadness makes them drink, and drink drives them mad.

While a little gentle philosophizing may be tolerable as a kind of hobby, many who are carried along by a usual routine and lulled by daily repetitions will resent any attempt to be driven to ultimate issues, especially if they are expected to act on what they find there. Socrates was condemned to death by the injustice of ordinary men, perhaps as much out of their exasperation with a nuisance as from any feeling that he was an enemy to established religion and the city.

Of course some things are better taken in our stride without halting, and nonsense has sometimes been recommended under the title of metaphysics: many of the terms thrown about have turned out to stand for idle entities. All the same perhaps it is to the credit of metaphysicians that they risk making fools of themselves—

> Two voices are there: one is of the deep,
> And one is of an old half-witted sheep—

Yet to start with, though later we may have to revise our views about the validity of bluff commonsense, a respect for the dogged and permanent convictions of unlettered folk who know the seasons, the plants, the animals, how to make a living and bring up a family, who face the problems of life and death without an anæsthetic, will make us suspicious of solemn abstraction and forced cleverness, of a mincing manner and an airyfairy quite out

c

of touch with the feel of things. There is little to be said for the
high fantastical when graciousness or colour or juice or common
humanity are lacking; the land of the jumblies but without any
warmth.

Metaphysics is undoubtedly hard, but is arduous rather than
tortuous, difficult rather than complex. It is like having to learn
a rhapsody by Liszt without having to explain the enigmas of his
personality. The experts who take it as a specialized topic of
research adapt or invent a technical language for their own convenience; even so the vocabulary is not so esoteric as that of some
of the other sciences, though the difficulty is also present that
words are sometimes used in one sense and sometimes in another.
Many problems are refined in ways that need not engage the
general reader.

Nevertheless the heart of metaphysics lies close and responsive to the ordinary motions of our life. It beats in unison with
sensation; only minds embodied can be metaphysical minds.
Wreck a physical track, and metaphysics itself may be deranged,
as the conduct of operations in the campaign of Leipzig was
impaired by the upset of Napoleon's secretions. Everybody willy-
nilly lives in a metaphysical world and uses its concepts, and, fail
or succeed, he tries to rough out some sort of plan from his reflections. All conscious things, says St Thomas, implicitly know
God in everything they know. Metaphysics is like theology, not
a clandestine occupation, and like theology too it is resilient,
pushed down in one place only to spring up in another. A particular system may be displaced, but the effort to formulate a general
doctrine is unflagging so long as men live at their proper stretch.
The experts perhaps are not the best witnesses of this attempt and
its success, but we should be put off by their researches no more
than we are put off our food because of the faddists, off sport
because we are not professionals, or off religion because we are not
reverends.

Patience and candour are demanded if we are to be explicit
metaphysicians, also the ability of going rather quiet inside, of
not asking too much at a time, of being content to settle one question before passing on to the next, of resisting the temptation to
pass slashing judgements or to espouse a cause before the
issue is really appreciated. The spirit blows not in the great

strong wind, nor the earthquake, nor the fire, but in the still
small voice. It is through the cracks, someone has said, that
ecstasy creeps in. We shall find that the more we enlarge our
knowledge the more we extend and expose the surface of our mind
to a surrounding mystery. As in mysticism so in thought, we
grow in the *docta ignorantia*. Metaphysics cannot be mugged up
like the dates of the Kings of England. One must slide into it
slowly and let it become a habit of mind. Huxley is supposed to
have ripped the heart out of Suarez during one afternoon in the
library of Glasgow University, and there was another student who
spent a good quarter of an hour reading up thomism. That might
suffice for a system, though one might doubt it, unless the learner
were a Hampdenshire Wonder. Metaphysics requires less of an
effort of concentration; it is the habit of contemplating things in
their highest and most universal causes.

Unafraid of the name, then, let this study be approached with
the reminder that it was called metaphysics because Aristotle's
treatise comes after his books on the physics, and with the reflection that the body, though seemingly so warm and companionable, is the principle of death and division; and that the mind,
though seemingly wan and remote, is the principle of human
living and unity. We shall begin with the general subject matter,
namely being as such, not this thing or that thing, not particular
aspects or references, but being as being, considered in the most
general context. Beneath the abstraction lurks the concrete thing,
but that for the moment we must affect to leave. We forget for a
while the accustomed world of particular incidents and try to make
ourselves at home with the widest generalizations; away from all
knots and tangles, away from lines and string; instead—just *isness*.

6. *The Prospect Before Us*

The first enquiry will be about the validity of the enunciation,
that being is. The rest of the volume will be occupied with meditations on the problem of knowledge, that is on the enunciation
that *being is true*. Afterwards we may be able to draw on the
riches that lie behind the apparent poverty of the statement by
working its necessary implications, properties, and consequences:
how being can be one yet manifold, how surprising and yet dis-
playing an intelligible security.

Such technical terms as *potentiality* and *actuality* are occasions for elaborate controversy from which we can lie well back, but they are also rewarding to any sensitive thinker who is content to catch a hint of things round the corner. They should be treated like notes of music or lines of poetry, able to transport us beyond our powers of criticism. After that we shall come to the analogy of being, a doctrine difficult in itself, but promising a glimpse of excitement in rest, an intermittent beam on the darkness of matter, a method of discovery that is scientific without forgetting colours and scents and sounds. Then finally can be considered the divisions of things as they interact on one another according to the various categories of causality.

The problem of knowledge may be treated as a topic for logic. This would require a close analysis of the difference between categoric and conditional propositions, which is not to our purpose, for we are concerned with a kind of residue irreducible to logic, namely the reference to an existent. Nor are we going to treat the problem in terms of psychology, that is by considering the concept of knowledge as a vital adjustment to our supposed surroundings, though of course such considerations cannot be excluded altogether. The emphasis is on metaphysics; we are out to elucidate the general conditions of knowing. Here also we shall avoid as far as possible the debate about the status and implication of our general ideas. In the person of Abelard the old scholastic philosophy rose in protest against the nominalism of Roscellinus, to whom ideas were merely breaths of sound; only later to react equally against the overrealism of William of Champeaux to whom individuals were rather like so many lumps of meaning. We shall affirm that types are real, but not that they comprehend everything real.

Three patches have to be cleared: the outside world, the self, and the absolute. As presented according to the main patterns of perennial and instructed human experience, the outside world is more or less fitted for that search into the penultimate what? and why? called natural philosophy by the ancients. We shall begin by taking its main lines for granted. As regards the self, which seems to reproduce within itself a world outside, our topic is in the validity of cognition, approached not by a departmental enquiry into this or that form of knowledge, but in a description of its general characteristics. What is held by knowledge is more our interest than what knowledge does, its content more than its character as a useful adaptation to environment.

Behind all these questions looms the problem whether know-ing as knowing contains anything apart from a mental state, with the trailing fear that whatever happens in the mind is just a musing and a day dream. Phrased in various ways, the issue has been thrust into the rôle of the first and fundamental question of critical metaphysics. Some have thought that until it is squarely faced all our reflections are so many embroiderings on a doubt and making do with a pretence. Others point out, and with some force, that as often stated it is really a false problem; certainly the ensuing discussion can be as unavailing as the emotions of the compassionate *Generall* referred to by Donne who looking upon his great Army, from a hill, fell into a bitter weeping, upon this consideration, that in fiftie or sixtie yeares hence, there will not be a man of these who fight now, alive upon the earth.

CHAPTER II

VAGUE CERTAINTIES

IF we make the longest cast, neither watching this under our eyes nor listening to that at our ears, if we disregard the variety, the shot silk, the shadow, the fleeting glimpse, the echoing strain, the sidelong glance of suspicion, the twinge of pain, if we start without elaborate technique, without psychology and sociology, even without mysticism, if we reach out to what is most vague and yet most certain, if we take a deep breath and soar into the high thin air or burrow into the bowels of the earth—it amounts to the same, if we leave everything that is customary and solid and coloured, what then is left for us to think about?

Is, first; and then, *is not.*

7. *Being*

There they are, the original counters of thought—something and not-something, or preferably, being and non-being, for at this stage the latter pair of terms are less taxing to the mind though more sonorously ringing in the ear. Whereas *something* hints at something else, a doctrine of pluralism that has yet to be established, here the term *being* merely states an object of attention. *Not-anything* similarly certifies an absence of definition that presumably in some cases might be expected, and so does *not-something.* But *non-being* and *nothing* merely express an absence of reality. Positive and negative neat, the two great ends of fate, being and non-being, reality and non-reality, their opposition is less pretentious and at the same time more profound than the contrast between this and not-this, a take it or leave it more final than the customary alternatives of this and that, left and right, day and night, male and female, right and wrong.

The ultimate conflict has been reached, though uttered in our dry logical fashion when we think *is* and then express the denial, *is not.* What a personal crisis is here, though not necessarily directed to the question of Hamlet's soliloquy. This book is an attempt to rouse some of the echoes. But for a space we remain vague. Later on we shall see if we can work from the general affirmation of being and its corresponding negation to the conviction that we can say *something*, meaning one real thing amid a multitude of others; but that must wait until we consider the course of general metaphysics after having established the validity of its early steps. In the meantime the word *something* is used to mean merely anything at all: the flimsiness of the concept is noted partly as a reassurance that we are not going suddenly to solidify it and then swiftly enlarge on the picture of a host of real objects, acting on one another and including in their number some with minds somehow able to possess the others.

Being is not an assumption, as will be seen later; the first meaning in the first motions of our minds, it cannot be dislodged. We cannot unthink it; we cannot think without it. We do not find it by sifting the evidence, for it is in all the evidence. We think being as object; it may turn out merely to be a projection of ourselves, though in passing we note that it appears primitively as an object pitted against us.

It will not pass without comment that already we are acquiring the habit of taking for granted that each of us is one thing surrounded by many others, the so-called fallacy of simple location, and that what is felt to happen in us may be supposed to happen also in them, the so-called pathetic fallacy. But indeed to avoid this manner of speaking is impossible if we would speak at all: we need not shuffle before the rules of linguistic logic, but should boldly recognize the dogmatisms that crowd in on everything we say; and though for the present we are concerned solely with one dogmatism, namely the affirmation of being, it wakens many echoes. There is no statement however simple that cannot but be taken in many different senses. That is to be expected if a common theme runs through all the variations. Language that is both single-minded and sensitive does not pick a cautious way from stilted premisses, but runs at ease and tosses away the crutches of semantics, as may be seen in the parallelisms of the Hebrew psalms and the figures of Spanish proverbs; many of our own phrases, such as *hungry soil* and *tender ship*, are tributes to the analogies within the simple meaning of being to which a metaphysician of all people should show himself particularly responsive.

Ambiguity has to be taken in our stride if we are to arrive any-
where at all. We should admit that our premisses are anticipated
by our conclusions, and that the edges of one concept may in the
concrete overlap those of many others. Though our reasoning
processes always tend to work round in curves we can yet without
vicious circles display our inferences and straddle meanings with
tolerable accuracy. The mind has hearing as well as sight, it
should listen to rhetoric while it observes the figures of argument,
and if at first there is only the score nevertheless in the end there
may be music.

Making allowance for imagery, then, we affirm that being is
presented as object of mind. What on earth it is, why that is
another matter; the time has not yet come to investigate the
doubts that rise on reflection, pausing over some of the more
vexing aspects of the problem of knowledge, fixing every shadow
and suspicion, perhaps even inducing the mood of doubting
whether anything at all exists apart from ourselves. The first
affirmation is easier than the subsequent reflection. I can cross the
Elbe all right, said Kutusov gloomily, yet watch me recross it
presently and with a bloody nose. But for our first excursion we
must get cracking, like an armoured division when the minefields
have been bridged and the crust of the defence broken. Events
and second thoughts may cause us to try to pull out and see if we
can begin again. But always the start must be from being as
object: there is no alternative if we are going to start at all.

Now this object, whether it consists of me alone and my
dreams, or whether it is the pervasive stuff of which I am a ripple
or shade or rustle, or whether it be multiplied in a universe of
many things of which I am one, this reality of *isness* is in some way
present to my attention. There is a reference to it in all my
thoughts—about the Balearics, the Venerable Bede, taxation, children's voices, flamingoes, the weather, everything. The lees left
in every experience?—even that is not accurate, for it is more than
the leavings; there is nothing being does not wholly possess and
penetrate from the first stirrings of human attention.

Sometimes existence may flash on us, and we look up to see
who makes the general gesture of being throughout the world.
'If I should aske the Basilisk,' cries Donne, 'how camest thou by
those killing eyes, he would tell me, Thy God made me so; and if

I should aske the Slowe-worm, how camest thou to be without eyes, he would tell me, Thy God made me so. The Cedar is no better a glasse to see God in, than the Hyssope upon the wall; all things that are, are equally removed from being nothing; and whatsoever hath any beeing, is by that very beeing, a glasse in which we see God, who is the roote, and the fountaine of all beeing.'

But let us back away from that vision and content ourselves with the stubborn presence of *is* in everything we think. If we reject being we shall then be led to adopt what Tierney thought was the very simple duty of an Opposition—to oppose everything and propose nothing. But even that would be denied us; except for acting a part, we could lay no claim to say anything of any significance at all. We might be busy contriving the necessities and amenities of a life quite without meaning, but we could hold no views or register no reasoned disapproval. We should be like the old Greek whose wisdom at the end led him to remain steadily mum. Sheer scepticism cannot even affirm its universal doubt; what it can do is to put up a sheerly destructive defence, fighting as Hitler will promise to do, and pulling the world down in its defeat.

'It is one thing,' observes Locke, 'to show a man that he is in error, and another to put him in possession of truth.' So instead of trying to refute universal scepticism we are trying to find out if a world and its plan can be discovered in the fundamental stuff of consciousness. We may find in the end that the task is beyond us, but there is no point in raising difficulties before their time or resigning ourselves to disappointment before we have properly stated our hopes.

8. Truth

Without a conviction that it has an object other than itself the mind is like a fleet without a base. For the present, however, all that we confess is that the mind has an object, and that this object has some intelligibility. This is the ultimate concession, from which the reason cannot budge, and beyond which we cannot go. Were there no such end, remarks St Thomas, we should stray indefinitely without any goal or any stop. Consequently no science would be possible; and, he adds, that which the mind originally conceives and into which it resolves all other conceptions is being.

At this stage, when the problem of knowledge is stripped to the gantline, to load to capacity such terms as object, intelligibility, meaning, real, will not be necessary. Neither need we suspect that what is true or cognized is different from what is. The separation may be forced on us, but let us wait until it comes: we are not thereby committed to the commonsense doctrine that I am a fairly solid object in a crowd of other more or less solid things, all occupying a part of space, some of us standing on firm ground, most of us bathed in air and water or surrounded by soil.

The object of which we speak is less firmly concrete and rounded; the intelligibility is less vivid, but also less variable. Whittle and whittle away as much as you can or care, criticize and doubt every current dogmatism, find your world going strange and swimmy and mistly, live in a phantasmagoria, a dream or a nightmare, a picture by Fuseli and not by Stubbs, and, so soon as you go beyond the mere sensations of the situation and bear yourself as a man in the excitement or the boredom, you either find some meaning or are pulled up short by the lack of it.

To be puzzled and resentful is evidence of the mind's constitution and expectations. The play of life may be accepted as a farce or watched as a heavy melodrama, enjoyed as a comedy or suffered as a tragedy, but all these employ categories of meaning: the play always becomes a morality. However topsy-turvy the scene, poor the joke, perverted the arrangement of circumstances, however lamentable the consequences, a complete lack of meaning in a human situation is incredible. Otherwise there would be no condemnation, no, nor any human tolerance and endurance; no rebellion, no human anger, but merely spleen. Some semblance of connection always appears, not seldom disguised. Relations are judged to be awry only by some sense of fitness.

Appetite is evidence for what may be, *desiderium naturale numquam inane*—'for amiss he were made, who was made not for joy.' This does not mean that we shall be inevitably gratified, but that our longings are not pointless. There is no drive without a goal, no urge without an object. To dismiss an argument on the grounds that it is wish-fulfilment thinking is really a doubled-edged discommendation. A need for intelligibility is inherent in our thinking; the want is explicable only if there is a meaning some-where. Most of us can invent most of the time, but not all of us all of the time. It remains to be seen whether the general object is merely a starting point, or whether we can work it up into a rational plan that meets a more entire situation. For the present we are merely concerned with the embryo of human knowledge.

I think, and in my thought is *being*, or thingness. Vagrant and unattached it may be, whimsical, wavery, heartless and all out of focus. Cruel it may prove, and bad if you like. The egg may be addled, but at least there was an egg. But reality is there, and our job is to meet and master it. At first it may seem one with us, and then afterwards it may seem our opponent, and then later it may seem part of us. But whatever it is, we should resolutely observe its immanent justice and embrace it. We should not be put off by imaginations and fears, some of them perhaps not base-less, but these we should sort out later. The reality we find may not be the sort of reality we should chose for ourselves; the natural appetite which prophesies it is not personal taste and choosiness.

The stage of affirming that this object is an *outside* thing to us, or even that it is an *other*, has not yet been reached. Though the situation may be imagined as one of simple location, our thoughts are not committed to the picture of pieces of matter dispersed in space. The White Knight looked surprised at the question. 'What does it matter where my body happens to be?' he said. 'My mind goes on working all the same. In fact, the more head-downwards I am, the more I keep on inventing new things.'

In anticipation we may observe that there is an element in our articulate consciousness we recognize as not completely identical with us. At least a mental distinction is set up when an object of thought is deliberately considered. It is possible, too, that the subject-object polarization corresponds to the subject-predicate polarization at a level lying below the logical analysis of pro-positions. Without sounding these depths we are content to say that there is an object of mind, without deciding whether it is a spark from within the thinking subject, or a beam from a more general mind lighting on our limited centre of consciousness, or a luminous form existing independently of our mind and perhaps shining in sub-mental stuff.

9. *First Object*

The original element in our thinking is being at its most abstract; aloof from individual occurrences, as in the physical sciences; from motion and colour and scent and feel, as in the mathematical sciences; from shape and size and number. In the early phase of metaphysics when being is taken flatly as being, an object neither tricky like a poltergeist nor supposititious like curvature without line or snubness without nose, nor drifting and unattached, like being in love with love, but firm and level and serene, it is a tranquil expanse covering all that is and can be, all that is thought or can be thought, the common reality of everything, and yet, as will be seen, surprisingly diversified and intimate to the heart of each thing as well.

A man may start, and profitably too, from an unanxious acceptance of the world about him as it seems to be presented through his senses and as recommended by other men of his tradition and nation, and particularly by those who seem to make a good living out of it. When he travels into other regions, either of geography or of psychology, the accustomed shapes and patterns may vary, and what he has been brought up to believe may seem strange and dreamlike, fairy-tales of his youth. Yet even so a sense of hard fact according to the environment in which he now finds himself may still provide an active preparation for his thought and prevent a theoretical worry. However for the present we are trying to manage without even that presupposition, we are not starting from ascertained facts, but are trying to begin from what is left when all that is particular and peculiar and vivid and painful and pleasurable has been drained away, from what is left when all the hard particles of our experience have been dissolved. We are taking merely *isness*, the essence of is, in the least pretentious sense of the word.

How puffed out and mighty this participle of the verb *to be* can be made to appear. *Being* and *the Absolute*—what a pomp of terms. Yet both are easier to understand than *The Thing* and *The Relative*: how baffled the reason really is by happenings, and what teasing problems surround the philosophy of relations. There are more mysteries in natural than in metaphysical science, more surprises in practical than in theoretical morals. Being is not so grand as it sounds. For even if we saw all its facets in a single metaphysical vision we should not thereby possess the Good, or be good men in the usual sense of the term, or hold the complete and rounded substance of any one thing. For in our minds the mode of being is abstract, carrying with it neither an aesthetic experience through the senses nor deep intimacy with anything. It may not be profound, it is certainly not poignant, it may be smug, yet it is pretty inclusive.

Nothing is excluded, or rather not anything is excluded. For though the metaphysician is most abstract and therefore wears the air of peering at one select side to all facts, his drive nevertheless is to the whole; the only term he refuses to face is the *nothing*. Everything else receives at least a sidelong glance. If being penny is plain, twopence it is coloured. And to the metaphysician entire belongs the exciting task of sounding the analogies running through all being and descending down even to the local varieties. Dante Gabriel Rossetti told Whistler he was going to put a sonnet into paint. 'Then why not paint it?' was the answer. If Whistler was out of humour with the looseness, the metaphysician cannot be so precious and exact. He should allow for any evidence, logical consistency, sublimity, practical appeal, primitive squalor, even utility and intellectual seediness; entering into all conflicts of contraries in order to find their common ground, loving both *L'Allegro* and *Il Penseroso*. The only rejection he is bound to make is of one of two contradictories. He refuses non-being or nothing, and is left with being.

The nothing is not what does not exist, but what could not exist, what is chaotic and contradictory at core. This is the nothing *de jure*, the metaphysical emptiness. It is not the historical nothing, the nothing *de facto*, such as the British expedition to Finland that never came off, which is as much—or as little— inside the object of metaphysics as the expedition to North Africa that did. The metaphysician is as much concerned with abortive or improbable facts as with successful facts, as much with sea-serpents as with giant congers. His first emphasis, however, is apart from facts altogether, his original phase is with the isness of is: but this is temporary, for the science of general notions is designed to destroy itself in a more adult mode of knowledge. To prolong the abstraction would be to open a dangerous fissure between essential meanings and properties on one side and existential

incidents and events on the other, and would reduce metaphysics
to the state of a formal analysis of meaning and leave the empirical
sciences merely as tidy recordings of what happens to happen.

Nevertheless at the start the abstraction made by metaphysics
from the things that are happening about us may be heightened.
How difficult it is to write with interest of this initial separation
from the tumult of experience, how easy to present primary being
as dead and flat, without spring or pulse.

Just being as such.

Of course it may be said, why try to make it interesting? If
it be taken as an undeniable beginning, that is surely enough to
lay a foundation, the bread and butter before the cakes at nursery
tea. But our anticipations will not allow us to treat even mere
being like that; from the start the interest must rise from within
it, like sap from a root, or beauty from health. All truth is from
the Logos, and this, as Clement of Alexandria taught, is the New
Song; ever old and ever young. Though abstract and general,
metaphysics yet comes like 'a basin of nice smooth gruel, thin,'
we may add with Emma's father, 'but not too thin.'

There is no need to lead off in the manner of the bishop's
sermon, 'I feel a feeling which I feel you all feel.' Were the
philosopher to stay with the vague platitude of being, he might
well appear a dull fellow, ponderously affirming the airy and
labouring at the obvious, stirring and stirring again the grey un-
substantial pudding in which there is not spice or aroma, not even
the sparkle of a threepenny-bit of interest. But it is only in the
last century or so that philosophers have recovered the forbidding
characteristics of Chrysippus and acquired a lack lustre reputation,
and many of them have not deserved it.

Geniality is one attitude and bonhomousness another, and no
more than religion should philosophy need the recommendation
that its practitioners can be eminent in other walks of life, as if
frequenting the sacraments is confirmed by the example of a
famous baseball player or religious faith because professed by the
father of antiseptic surgery. All the same it is undeniably heart-
ening to recall that Hippias could boast at an Olympiad that he
made all his own clothes and that Newman was an excellent man
of business, that Montaigne was Mayor of Bordeaux and that
Collingwood could handle a boat and write with authority of

Roman Britain. Perhaps being is suppler than it seems, and metaphysics not such a tight little secret after all.

10. *An Advance*

What is is, and there's an end on't—but there is no end to it. The statement has already touched off a train of metaphysical thinking. A necessity has been affirmed. Though we may have intended no more, in effect we have gone beyond the simple registration of an occurrence. Unlike blotting paper absorbing blots, we have reacted with a judgement: what is—is; what is not—is nothing. Being is not non-being; perhaps something is not something else. Behind the judgement even when it is bound up with a particular event—'there, there, child, there it is, and you can't undo the past'—a more general recognition is implied, namely that is is is, and that is not is is not, or that is not is not is.

These truisms may be flat, like the definition of law travestied by Bentham, 'a rule of conduct for those who are to observe it, prescribed by those who prescribe it, commanding what it commands, and forbidding what it forbids.' But say if they turn out to support much else? Foundations need not be ornamental nor engage the attention of others besides architects and structural engineers. Commonplaces have been so questioned in recent times that sophistication may now claim some credit for professing them. But say if they are also openings and promises, and say if from them the mind can play in philosophy like a puppy in the snow? St Thomas compares wisdom to a game, and indeed at its best philosophy is too serious to be solemn. But the time has not yet come to look around and stretch ourselves.

Already a good start has been made with the judgement that being is not non-being, something not nothing, and nothing not something. These convictions, indispensable for reasoned activity, are formulated in what are called the first principles which appear at the dawn of thought.

Two are traditionally enumerated, namely the principle of identity and the principle of contradiction. The former is affirmative, the latter negative, but both amount to saying that there is some reason in what we think, not necessarily a prim and didactic regularity nor a well-taped state of affairs, but at least the intelligent sensibility found in Chinese Sharawadgi.

The principle of identity runs, what is—is. A less bald translation of its correlative, the principle of contradiction, according to material conditions states that it is impossible for the same thing both to be and not to be in the same way at the same time. As a longer and more local sentence and as having a more dialectically decisive sound it is in commoner use. Neither the principle of identity nor the principle of contradiction is just a meaningless repetition, or, as St Thomas says, *nugatorie dicitur*, a futile saying. Though tautological in appearance, in reality it does not say the same thing twice over, for it carries a note of necessity, a tone of inevitability and conviction, as when in a more particular situation it is said that boys will be boys.

Once we have consciously assented to the truth of the first principles of thought we are reaching to the fullness and turning away from the void. And in this first flush we should not feel impeded by the problem of knowledge which has hag-ridden philosophy for two centuries. Moreover we are buckling to being as such without drawing bounds to our knowledge. Doubts may afflict us later, looking back we may wonder how we have got where we are; but there is no return. Nor can we start with qualifications. It is not like crossing a bog where we can step forward hesitantly and cautiously; we find ourselves up to the neck from the start. Thinking is like breathing or swimming, we may regret that we are alive or in the water, but on the supposition that we are doing what we are doing there can be no speculation as to the reality of our start. If we are in thought then we are within the object of thought, and this in its most general terms is being. Epistemology or the criticism of knowledge may be the first chapter of metaphysics, but a dogmatic preface is required.

But before seeing whether we can enlarge this most generalized object, or rather if we can develop it from within, growing a layer there, then taking it off to look underneath, then replacing it and growing another layer, let us briefly refer to the doubts that may arise almost from the beginning, leaving metaphysics 'like a sick eagle looking at the sky.'

11. *A Sham Problem?*

Being is: that is the first fresh metaphysical proposition—no vain repetition, for by saying *is is is,* a doctrine is advanced and problems begin. The same term is repeated thrice, but the second term and third add force to the first time of publication, and the whole carries a meaning and an accent of necessity lacking in any of the parts. *Is* alone is merely an evocation, almost like *ah!* But *is is is* strikes an attitude and takes up a position. Where does the addition come from? Perhaps only from our minds, reading inventions into experiences to give them shape; perhaps from elsewhere.

That special problem however can be postponed, except to docket for future reference the suggestion that perhaps thinkage and thingage are the same, and that whether everything physical is ultimately mental or whether contrariwise everything mental is ultimately physical matters very little in the end. The Jesuit and his Franciscan friend were both heavy smokers, and they both wanted a cigar while they performed their obligatory spiritual exercises; the latter requested permission to smoke during his devotions and was refused, whereas the other, more wise in his generation, asked if it were laudable to pray while he smoked.

It all depends from which direction you look at the scene. To start with a cleavage between thought and thing is asking for trouble, a premature pessimism for which unfounded optimism is no cure. When the concept is treated as an imitation rather than a continuation, and when the mind is placed on one side and reality apart on the other and you then try to make them correspond the problem becomes insoluble. The mistake lies in starting with a gap, rather than in watching distinctions develop within what is already given and afterwards seeking to keep it within the bounds of this system of reference. This opposition between think and thing was the radical problem of philosophy for close on two centuries until students began to suspect that perhaps they were asking a pseudo-question. For in trying to isolate real being from all consciousness we are like the man who concluded that the sun was not very useful for it only shone when it was already light; and in seeking a critical principle that would establish the first principles of thought we were crying for the moon: the same man said that the moon was much more important because at least it did shine during the night.

Of course there comes a moment when the question must be faced, how the thinking subject and the object perceived are united.

D

Or rather we must squint back at it, for our minds are made to gaze out. But in any case the enquiry is psychological rather than epistemological; in other words, the union is its own evidence in the sense that its existence is inescapable, while all that remains is for its character and implications to be elucidated by analogies. Is it thinkable that two things can enter one another and be possessed by one another without suffering any real change? Are there motions exhibiting such phenomena? Though enhancing and advancing them in the scale of biological progress, in what sense is cognition irreducible to neurological processes? Knowledge itself is a fertile field of study without overt reference to the philosophy of doubt. And if the doubt has to be opened and a purely epistemological path pursued, should it not be assumed to begin with that there is a union between knower and known, a primitive presence preceding reflection and open to critical examination only in the light of evidence supplied by itself? In other words, that criticism should be reserved for the construction that we build on it. The collapse of a building is a demonstration of the fundamental canons of good architecture; the sceptical destruction of philosophical systems a tribute to the force of first principles.

'Alice knocked and rang in vain for a long time, but at last a very old Frog, who was sitting under a tree, got up and hobbled slowly towards her; he was dressed in bright yellow, and had enormous boots on.

' "What is it, now?" the Frog said in a deep hoarse whisper.

'Alice turned round, ready to find fault with anybody. "Where's the servant whose business it is to answer the door?" she began.

' "Which door?" said the Frog.

'Alice almost stamped with irritation at the slow drawl in which he spoke. "*This* door, of course!"

'The Frog looked at the door with his large dull eyes for a minute: then he went nearer and rubbed it with his thumb, as if he were trying whether the paint would come off; then he looked at Alice.

' "To answer the door?" he said. "What's it been asking of?" He was so hoarse that Alice could scarcely hear him.

' "I don't know what you mean," she said.

' "I speaks English, doesn't I?" the Frog went on, "or are you deaf? What did it ask you?"

' "Nothing!" Alice answered impatiently, "I've been knocking at it!"

' "Shouldn't do that—shouldn't do that—" the Frog muttered. "Wexes it, you know." Then he went up and gave the door a kick with one of his great feet. "You let *it* alone," he panted out, as he hobbled back to his tree, "and it'll let *you* alone, you know." '

Not a few philosophers have landed themselves in the embarrassment of Alice at the door, with some of the dogmatists cast for the rôle of the Frog. Once we expect to find a door and not an opening, and once we allow doubts about the friendly responsiveness of mind and object at the origins of knowledge, the stage is set for one side or the other to be suppressed. On a rough division we may say that some have banked on the mind and subject, and others on the thing and object. Until they were driven back from consciousness into the unconscious, the idealists or mentalists were among the former: being is being perceived, *esse est percipi*; everything is mind-stuff. Others, the materialists and positivists, preferred the object, even to the total elimination of a conscious subject exhibiting any functions that could not be explained by the categories of mechanics. Like many others, the contest began in the days of the Greeks.

Here is found the most profound application of the either-or fallacy, or the false alternative. Instead we must seek to retain both subject and object and, though without attempting proof at this stage—if indeed a positive proof can ever be forthcoming—maintain that there is a mental state and a distinct physical object, and that the two are different yet both come from the same stable. The presumption is against a forced and premature antithesis; our suspicions should be roused by the downright issue of one or the other. On this, as on other topics, we should prefer to say *both*, for both have a pressure of evidence, and then bend ourselves to set the opposites in the active co-operation of a synthesis. We should adopt the character of the Trimmer, who equally hates to be under the oppression of wrangling sophistry on one hand, or the short dictates of mistaken authority on the other; moreover we should not be ashamed of the name, for our Trimmer, concludes Halifax, 'is so satisfied of the truth of these Principles that he will neither be Bawled, Threatened, Laught nor Drunk out of them.'

But to return to where we were. When we say *is is is*, perhaps the advance, for advance it is, comes from our mind and takes place in our mind. No matter. Perhaps it is only an advance in paper logic, but in real truth a repetition. Still no matter, though a bore. These pages will attempt to show that a bore may be turned to interest and profit.

Were our minds completely simple they would be content—philosophically speaking—to see *Is* and utter it in silence: visionaries speak little when it comes to the point, though they are frequently off it: pure intelligences, as Augustine says, do not entertain *volubiles cogitationes*, the chatter of thought. Our minds, however, are partial and complex in their consciousness; they divide, they unite, they pass judgements, they try to explain themselves to themselves and, what is more embarrassing, to others. Apart from the fundamental dualism of subject and object multiplied and twinkling from a thousand wavelets, there is also at work the logical dualism of the subject of a sentence and its predicate, ever being capped by a progression of fresh series as every predicate itself becomes a subject.

Yet, as already hinted, the subject of a sentence may be identified with the knowing subject considered as the object of rational enquiry, who mysteriously for a split second sets reality apart from himself in uttering the predicate, dividing himself from his world in a kind of metaphysical sacrifice, only to be reunited when through a living copula he identifies subject and predicate.

12. *Modest Beginnings*

The first principles of metaphysics do not produce fresh knowledge; there is no purely deductive construction from a simple datum to a universe in which we can live, no open sesame to the cave of riches. There is a limit to what contradictions can construct, for as often as not the appearance of productiveness comes from the method of opposition by an illicit transfer from contradictions to contraries, and then metaphysics assumes the condition of a dictatorship, under which anything not forbidden is obligatory. The tissue is more supple.

The body of philosophy itself, not to speak of humane knowledge generally, cannot be spun out from a few general principles assumed *a priori*, but must be generated from and be assimilated with experience. There is no substitute for the experimental method, no alternative to the lively and curious faculties of observation. Contemplation will not remedy the absence of hard work. Our reiteration of the axioms should not lead the reader to suppose that they are offered as ways of discovery; they are merely the points of the compass. In sticking by them we are speaking like the girl in the *Two Gentlemen of Verona*—

> I have no other but a woman's reason:
> I think him so because I think him so—

but there is much to be said for that; the sex of birth and death is the same for all, and does not enter into human argument.

Similarly first principles are not proferred as the explanation of any one thing, or even as throwing fresh light on a subject. Fundamental metaphysics does not here promise an adventure, but a test for what we already have; a solution in which other truths can be resolved. It may mother the other sciences, but its rôle is rather like that of Peter Simple's pelican: this bird feeds its young with its own blood—when fish are scarce. But fish are not scarce, they are all too numerous, and the mind with difficulty prevents itself from being swamped by the slithering and swelling shoals.

Metaphysics is humane and acceptable when it displays some sense of history. To expect high deduction to furnish what can come only from other ways of knowledge is a mistake; it is like treating the aristotelean syllogism as an instrument, not of exposition, but of discovery. Philosophy offers no clue to the secrets of the experimental sciences, nor is it a quick and convenient means of avoiding their arduousness. The sciences are not departments of metaphysics, for they have their own proper freedom, their own evidence, their own questions and answers, their own snags, and they can proceed in their own territory without raising philosophical issues as easily as a legal practioner can work without investigating the real nature of legal fictions or settling the theory of law.

Yet all the special sciences are subordinate to metaphysics inasmuch as the pattern of their processes and the inmost intelligibility of their objects should be backed by the evidence of being itself and conform to its consequences. This they must do under pain of dismissal, and the warning applies even to the paradoxical sections of mathematical physics. So though peculiar truths cannot be delivered from out of a general doctrine nevertheless they should be referable back to metaphysics. The particular sciences are, as it were, a marginal rather than an interlinear gloss to philosophy.

There are two reasons for this reference back, one negative the other positive. First it is sometimes necessary, especially in specialized research, to observe whether our processes and conclusions are consonant with the strict exigences of thought; if not, then they must be ruled out, anyhow so far as their theoretical validity is concerned, though they may have an interim value as occasions for practical advance, rather as gracelessness is the occasion for contrition. *O felix culpa* is not confined to theology, and temporary contradictions are part of the dialectic of science.

To serve as a kind of general check may be called the negative function of metaphysics. Yet there is also a positive function. The particular sciences are inherently sectarian. If they are to work in profitably with one another they have to be taken back behind their immediate premises or prolonged beyond their proper conclusions. Here the traffic of their connections will need to be regulated by a general code of science, and this, at its best, will offer more than a traffic plan. Lest it be thought that metaphysics adopts a policeman's lot when it descends from the height of its own contemplation, it should be remarked that the interplay of the sciences cannot be appreciated without a sense of analogy. The ideal scheme of the sciences may be represented as an interlocking series of triangles, or rather of arrow heads for the bases are not closed, mounting to a single apex; a body of truths grouped round a central massif.

As generous justice is not an affair of a legal code but of equity, so general metaphysics ceases to be a special subject. Though metaphysicians are not rarely a damp, metaphysics should foster without patronage the adventurous mind in the other sciences. Formal analysis is insufficient without a liberal dialectic to break down the barriers between the sciences and set them playing in communication with one another and with other ways of knowledge that are not strictly scientific. Philosophy should be like a university, which is not just a collection of different faculties but the home of a wide and generous spirit, offering not merely a choice of specialized techniques but a truly general education.

But to return again to the modest beginning of thought. Though they have been denied by thinkers of a sceptical turn of mind, whether anyone has succeeded in unthinking the first principles in his heart of hearts, or rather in his reason of reasons, is really questionable. They may be denied in so many words, the particular images they evoke may be rejected, especially when invested with the fashions of a philosophical period or modulated according to a philosophical system. Man is always bigger and better than the idols he sets up. There are certain moods of philosophical righteousness that call out to be scandalized by a man of spirit.

When, however, these principles are taken in their most general meaning they are present at least subconsciously in every rational judgement we pass. Whenever we think, even when we attempt to question them, they are implicitly assumed. We appeal to them when we would reject them, and gyrate in a vicious circle when we do deny them. From the outset the project is more impossible than speaking to a motion that speech is impossible. We philosophise even while we deny the validity of philosophy. Certainly both principles, the principle of identity and the principle of contradiction, are currently accepted in the transactions of everyday life, and we can spare ourselves the contortions of trying to unthink them.

All this may appear so much vague flourishing, but it cannot be avoided if we are to start modestly and soberly. No more easily than the air can this tenuous abstraction be thrust aside. It is not concentrated on an event, it does not get into its stride from a vivid realization of a particular thing, but from an indeterminate hint. Being and non-being, those are its poles, thing and nothing. Thing is not nothing, though what it is may not be what our commonsense takes it to be. Inescapable being!—were we told that it cannot be known we should still reason about it on that account, like the Greek philosopher who was asked why he wept for the death of his child, since the sorrow was in vain. 'I weep,' he replied, 'on that account.'

Chapter III

BUGABOOS

I HOLD an apple in my hand, my fingers feel its tacky polish. To workaday consciousness I am a more or less solid body and outside me there is another solid body, namely the apple; my reading of the situation has not changed since childhood. I may sturdily hold to this and from similar encounters multiply judgements that there are many other centres of energy outside me and other supports for sensible qualities, or I may conclude that all I know are certain perceptible manifestations of bunches of unknown forces, or I may be even more constrained and think that I merely register occasions for a series of charted references and all else is as cloudy and unattached as dreams are. But, whatever the mood, it is certain that I conceive the apple as more than nothing, in other words, as a being of some sort, or as belonging to being. Moreover I am expanding and grading within the general notion of being, for me-with-the-apple I conceive to be more than me-without-the-apple.

That these two complex terms are not identical is confirmed by the principle of contradiction. If the principle is doubted then the attempt to formulate explanatory and connected thoughts can be relinquished at once, and I may as well resign myself to exclamations and perhaps protests without meaning, an ill-humoured life of sensation. In conversation I should protest my inability to pass any judgement at all on the intellectual position of other people. I can purr and snarl, smile, grunt, or walk away. I cannot approve or condemn, agree or expostulate.

Such diffidence, in fact, is rare among sceptics. A more pugnacious set of thinkers never lived. They are like Tertullian writing a treatise on patience, or like a man who sits on the branch he is sawing off. Who more systematically destructive in their plans, who at greater rational pains to cut the ground from under the feet of reason, who more trenchant? Yet all the time they are putting up a bluff, for by their doubt their very weapons of

40

criticism have fallen from their grasp. For all their display of force and offensive passes, they have nothing to fall back on; they are like a convoy with a dummy battleship in the midst.

In truth, however, the famous and readable sceptics are not fundamental sceptics at all: they are people with an edgy sense of reasonableness and a character disinclined to suffer fools gladly, unscrupulous realists when it comes to the point; as often as not what they question are the conventions bred from fears and superstitions as well as from an easy and credulous disposition. Conversation is much easier with them than with the undogmatic sceptics in whom meanings ring no echoes.

13. *Various Realisms*

That the position—or prejudice—of full realism is adopted whenever it is not being consciously criticized will not pass unnoticed. That is an argument in its favour, almost decisive to most except professional critics, and even some of them respect the confirmation. It is instinctively adopted by most Europeans in the actual practice of successful living. But what is successful living? *Si monumentum requiris, circumspice!* for all is not in ruins after the destruction wrought by a rage possessed of powerful machinery and uncontrolled by the conviction that there is an overriding law of reality, a temperate code of decency. Still may be seen the measures accepted by the great builders of our culture, and by their parents, friends, and benefactors. There is an ease about a great period, not so much of bodily comfort as of intellectual dogmatism—China, Greece, Trajan's Rome, thirteenth-century France, sixteenth-century Spain, Whig England, and now?—both Moscow and the Mid-West represent confident causes. Live on a delusion hard enough, and so long as it is felt to be true there will be little psychiatric trouble; that comes from lack of security.

At least three stages of realism can be marked; sometimes they are recapitulated in the intellectual development of one individual thinker, sometimes they remain fixed and associated with different classes according to educational grading. They will be traversed briefly in the following pages. The first is the position of commonsense, direct and unworried; the second is more critical and reflexive, and perhaps more vulnerable, for it has

opened a flank; the third curves back on the first, and has recovered the security but not the temper, for now it is prepared to
take the debate beyond the bounds of workaday assents.

The position of commonsense is sometimes termed naive
realism, as much as to say that it is confident because unthinking,
usually by students who have penetrated deeply enough into the
critique of knowledge to have doubts but not far enough to have
dispelled them, and who can be like those individuals who have
separated themselves from the common convictions of the human
mass and thereby feel estranged and even guilty, more or less dis-
guisedly. Original realism seems to be the attitude of children
and of grown-ups of good general reading who take the world as
they find it, and would hesitate to call themselves metaphysicians.
It is the majority view, shared by people to whom fundamental
doubt has never occurred and by some who think doubting a
profitless proceeding, typified by the gesture of Dr Johnson
refuting the idealism of Berkeley outside Harwich Church.
'Though we are satisfied, says Boswell, his doctrine is not true it
is impossible to refute it. I shall never forget the alacrity with
which Johnson answered, striking his foot with mighty force
against a great stone, till he rebounded from it, "I refute it
thus." '

The second stage is both more technical and more haunted by
the slyness of the world, and is classically represented by the
classical theory of indirect realism, according to which our ideas
though supposed to be the objects of our knowledge are also
truthful representations of extra-mental objects. Or critical
realism may shed such a correspondence theory, and as in twentieth
century neo-realism, entering boldly into physiology, psychology,
and scientific method, may there attempt to refute subjectivism,
the doctrine that we cannot go beyond our own mental states.
No claim is made to enter metaphysics, in fact the name is rather
avoided, yet it is claimed that a rigorous analysis of the conditions
of cognition according to the categories of science discloses an
object that cannot be resolved into the modes of the subject
knowing. Not least valuable has been the spirited offensive
launched against some of the current assumptions of subjectivism,
mounted with a scientific terminology calculated to comfort the
plain man who has been brought up to think that the jargon of

learning and research must be opposed to his inherited and spontaneous convictions. It is as though detailed and highly scientific experiments on metabolism and nutrition had lead dieticians to assure us that a certain intake of fermented malt liquor is beneficial. The ordinary man is not ungrateful for the information.

At the third stage, the first conviction and the second analysis are gathered together into an abstraction beyond the range though not without the support of induction, and held more or less within the field of metaphysics. Some of the problems, for instance colour-blindness and other sense deceptions, previously a preoccupation at the second stage of enquiry, now slip out of the scene. This doctrine was not thoroughly explored and described by the great aristoteleans and thomists of the past, partly because they were strangers to the theoretical anxiety that has beset the European mind since the days of Descartes, partly because their insight into the existence of being led them to discount in advance the possibility that subsequent doubts could invalidate the force of their premisses, partly because the climate of their culture was clear and unromantic.

14. *From Realism to Doubt*

Most people take naive realism for granted without much reflection, if any. Even when its principles are questioned the habit soon slips back again into place and starts ticking over again almost automatically. Its assumptions run through idiomatic speech and the arguments at scientific gatherings, in the play of children and the colloquies of philosophers expressing their doubts. Even a congress of logical positivists cannot move without dialectic and rhetoric. Their thoughts cannot spring from nowhere, but are prompted by the pressure of a life-force and carried along a stream that follows the lie of the land.

Given proper care in the formulation of what we mean, it is held that our thoughts are pretty accurate reactions to a world outside. Perplexities may be entertained as speculative luxuries, but when all is said and done few of us are prepared really to think and act on them. When doubts are seriously suggested the reaction is to remark that if we don't ask nonsensical questions we shall be spared nonsensical answers.

If we wear the air of criticizing primitive realism, let us

confess in anticipation that commonsense is the embryonic
state of a realism that may be re-established after all manner of
sophisticated doubts have been undergone. Indeed, except for
filtering out certain impurities and dispensing with the cruder
images, it seems that the more prolonged and intensely philosophical the realist effort the more it tends to rejoin the movement
of simple directness. After all, metaphysics does not claim to
move into a fresh region populated by a new stock of things, it
does not extend the number of discoveries; what it can do is to
heighten and stabilize what we already have and to set conviction
in a stronger and steadier light of evidence. Though it intensifies
the truth metaphysical realism gains no new ground.

The attitude of commonsense is that I am one in a world of
many other things and am made aware of them through the
channels of the senses. The world is like a room, a very large
room chock full of pieces of furniture, all the pieces occupy a
place, and they can be moved about in space and thereby measured
by time. How solid we estimate the items, how fixed and detailed we paint the picture, will depend on our acquaintance with
modern theories of physics. Many will find no need to revise their
first valuation even when they are told, and see no reason to dis-
believe, that if we had microscopic vision a hawthorn tree would
be seen as particles very much like the cloud of midges dancing
under its boughs, though rather more closely packed together.

The things about us are credited with certain qualities imagined as forces able to produce a qualitative change in us. Sugar
is really sweet, dropped in the coffee it will soften the bitterness
and produce a pleasant sensation in our palate. We are not so
certain that such qualities can be scientifically investigated without translating them into another medium, and so we chart them
as quantities according to a convention of science and put them
into a mathematical notation. In the same spirit we may profess
that the best symbolic expression of the stark and subtle con-
tending forces in life is a cricket match. But the things which
impinge on us, whatever the mental construction we choose to
put on them for the sake of scientific registration, are considered
to exist independently of our thinking about them. We regard
ourselves as arriving on a scene that is already occupied and that
will remain so after we have gone.

And the tree
Continues to be
When there's no-one about in the quad.

But when we escape from this world of brutal facts and the
usual grid of measuring them, perhaps because we are suffering
from a high temperature or some glandular disturbance or nervous
disorder, or perhaps because we have forgotten our cursory readings of reality for our reveries or abstract analyses, then our world
becomes more wraithlike. We are such stuff as dreams are made
on: this may be felt when listening half-way through a sermon;
the preacher's face detaches itself and floats as a hazy disc through
a swirl and pronouns come adrift from periods and mock the
mind with mystery.

From their private seclusion of sensibility people can hold no
parley with one another. Dreams are incommunicable. Philosophical doubt, of course, is not just a piece of imagination that
has come unstuck, yet its results are not dissimilar. The mind is
no longer anchored or secured to a world not of its own making,
though the consequences should not be exaggerated, at any rate
the practical consequences. Many can continue to live fairly satis-
factorily for longish periods as hollow men: I rouse myself from
the sermon, the philosophical doubter stirs himself from his
reflections, and both of us turn to the world of ordinary transactions and go through the motions of our ritual service. The
idealist drives as hard a bargain in the market as does the positivist; the sceptic is as downright in debate as the believer.

The world is the background to common hopes and fears, and
the occasions are comparatively rare when men are called on to
act as though it did not enclose their practical desires. Some, it is
true, have the conviction that surrounding us there is an unseen
spiritual world, either of values felt at moments of high experience or of real substances inferred by philosophical speculation;
others believe in a world of preternatural agents, of magic and
perhaps of terror, certainly of awe. Strangeness is not far to seek
when we are jerked from our routine. When we leave outward
seeming things, or they are taken from us, when we are forced to
turn inwards, how sliding and slippery and hard to hold down are
the objects we find.

Normally our thoughts and indulgences tend to work along certain grooves, and these we project into the lives of others. We judge them from their gestures and words to have feelings like our own, we interpret and may be we sympathize, but, if we are wise, we prepare ourselves against surprise at many seeming anomalies. We proceed with diffidence, for soon we discover that people are also very different from ourselves in their images and emotions; we all know what snow is, but how differently we regard it, and how in one lifetime what once was fun is now a nuisance. We may know attraction to the opposite sex, but we also wonder what on earth could have induced him or her to marry her or him. Then there are zanies and geniuses, peoples of other races and traditions, as the sensitive subaltern in India used to discover. Even with one close and companionable and chosen there is always the inaccessible you.

Though we read our own sentiments into the animals, and credit them with anger and pleasure, hunger and thirst, and the sycophantic and domesticated among them play up to our supposition that their affections are analogous to our own in similar circumstances, we yet lack the immediate tests to prove it. Even babies are not decent in the usual sense of the term, as is shown by the gleam in their eyes as they mark you merely as an opportunity of something they want from the centre of their moist sensations. Even in saying that much I am interpolating myself.

Notwithstanding the moments when we are shocked out of taking things for granted, the system of naive realism works very well in the main. We may exhibit a certain theoretical reserve, but in practice it presents the sort of world that we lay our money on.

Yet is this reserve just a passing mood? In their heart of hearts few are intrinsically dominated by commonsense. There is within a questioning and eager spirit, perhaps a spirit of irreverent folly, certainly a power of criticism capable of putting everything to the test, the quirk remarked on by St Thomas of wanting to affront a law just because it is a law and a good law. Some give it rein, and then perhaps draw back frightened at the prospect, and others spur on and find themselves landed in predicaments different from those of commonsense. A moral emergency may match this intellectual phase, and be followed by various attempts, either to go back to respectability and commonsense or, what is better, to call up commonsense in support.

We should avoid the relief when an anxious problem impends of coming to the decision that we shall make no decision. That serves very well in some practical difficulties but it is a bad rule for a philosophy. Criticism once started should be pressed vigorously to the finish. So the problem of the profound doubt as to the validity of knowledge has to be faced in its most general terms. It lies deeper than any particular case. To pick holes in our systems and habits here and there is neither difficult nor un-called for; the various instruments and means of knowledge have constantly to be checked and verified or renewed. Commonsense itself settles some cases, as when we recognize that the doctrine of original sin has nothing whatever to say against advances in obstetrics; a spirit of historical criticism does for others, as when we appreciate that it would never have occurred to the foundation members of the Church to treat the scriptures as a collection of divinely dictated definitions; others respond to the laws of evidence that can be appreciated by a jury; others again can be sorted out by the ordinary processes of science, though many of these require specialist treatment. But underneath these special cases may lurk a universal doubt about the ability of our con-sciousness to introduce us to a reality wider than ourselves.

Such a problem can be resolved only in the terms of a uni-versal and synoptic science. A specialized and particular line can-not reach it. Metaphysics is not carried pick-a-back by any other science, and hence, says St Thomas, it must itself dispute with anyone who would deny its premisses. Yet even he must admit something, otherwise he cannot be disputed with, though his reasonings may be disproved. What this something is has already been hinted at; the following pages will continue to circle round its nature.

In the event metaphysics may have to be abandoned, and the base established on a non-rational assent, an awareness of a non-mental reality, a conjunction with a concrete thing antecedent to reasonings, an existent unverifiable by the analysis of meaning. We throw ourselves on the turf, and press our body into the earth, while our fingers scrabble into a stuff beyond our statement and before our awareness. A metaphysician who adopts such a

position is like a theist who allows that the classical proofs for the
existence of God amount to little more than clarifications of a
fact he already holds for non-rational reasons. It is not an irrational position.

Even so, if we are going to reflect on the situation and talk
rather than sing about it, we must evaluate it in the terms used
by the scientific reason. A metaphysician need not feel at all
dashed if he finds that he is called to address himself to non-
rational objects: his embarrassment is not peculiar, but attends all
scientific enquiry into the bases and culminations of all the other
sciences. Much truth lies beyond the strictly reasoning habits.
The non-rational is not the irrational, any more than the tuning
up of the orchestra and the final dying chord are anti-musical;
what may be so are the preliminary programme-notes and the
premature applause.

After all it is only what one should expect, for any reasoning
is a series of thoughts between two ultimate terms of knowledge
whose edges go out of the series, a movement between stages
which open out into another world. Accordingly we can continue
to discuss the problem of fundamental doubt with at least the
confidence of a musical critic in addressing himself to a symphony.
If certain questions are asked then certain answers must be
attempted. It may be well that we have asked the question, if
only to show us why we need never ask it again.

The drift of philosophy may be decided either by community
influences or by the personal idiosyncracies or genius of a few
great thinkers or by both. In tracing the movement from realism
to doubt and then back to realism again it will be more interesting
if we attach the names of great philosophers to the various periods,
yet with some warnings. There is more in a man than in his
system, and then even his proposals cannot be tossed off in a few
phrases. So much should be said in fairness. Men have brooded
over their subject and suffered perhaps for their findings and to
treat their names as labels, to think that we can sum up their
conclusions in a proposition or even a paragraph would be an
impertinence. No man is merely a type, though a penalty of fame
makes him such—byronic or gladstonian as the case may be. In
philosophy perhaps Plato is at once the greatest name and the
greatest sufferer, as St Augustine is in theology; the epithet

thomist has sometimes been used as a shibboleth strange to the idiom of St Thomas. Causes and men are rather different; one may condemn communism and be warm to communists, one may be convinced of Catholicism and yet be out of sympathy with what Catholics do.

Moreover we have to be on our guard against reading philosophy according to the terms of the history of philosophy. A stock of information may go towards an honours degree, but acquaintance with the doctrines of philosophers will not guarantee our possession of a philosophy. To know about the arguments of great thinkers is no substitute for holding enduring conclusions from principles. We cannot live on other men's convictions. To know what Aristotle and St Thomas teach, this, exclaims Cajetan, himself one of the great commentators, is not to be wise yourself.

15. *Appearances Deceptive*

Far back in the history of thought the suspicion appears that perhaps there is no end and object of knowledge at all; it is a widespread reflection that things are not what they seem. Allowing for the danger of re-reading early fragments of philosophy in the light of what has been thought of since, the name of Heraclitus stands for an ever working myth as well as for a historical person. You cannot step twice into the same running stream, for new waters are ever flowing in upon you. We are familiar with singularity and instability, and express it in many ways: truth is like joy, 'whose hand is ever at his lips, bidding adieu,'— it will never be the same again—opportunity beckons but once—the butterfly pinned on the board is no longer the butterfly. No sooner has an affirmation been made on any real topic than it has already changed. Nothing is still. Every statement is therefore out to touch with reality, and is itself a rendering into another medium which is always changing; probably as bad a translation as *holy wholly holey* for *sanctus sanctus sanctus*.

What we think now is not what *is* but what *was*. It might be urged that a past reality was something and we can live with a timelag in our knowledge by a kind of continuous memory. Small comfort, for a *has been* can be known only through an *is*. What is there to know if everything far from being on the point of going away has never been on any point at all, though well we

E

know it has gone away? Strangely the scepticism bred from such a lively apprehension of change may be extremely realist in temper, unless read in the interpretation of Protagoras. He thought the principle that all is becoming so relative to the subject that everything is equally true. But in general the temper of the philosophy of the flow is not to deny reality so much as to question our power of seizing it, at anyrate by an act of the reason. What is attacked is the pseudo-permanence of rational affirmations, what may be encouraged is living in the present, either according to the strain of existentialism or with the easier hedonism of crowning ourselves with roses before they wither.

Swinging to the other extreme we meet the name and myth of Parmenides. Every man of sensibility and intelligence surely has Heraclitus and Parmenides within him: from the scraps of their writings that remain, we can fill out a philosophy. Their sayings wake echoes in every mind. Parmenides stands for the type that believes that the only certainties are the fixed things, the enduring laws and stable meanings. Does the world appear to change and does change defy rational definition? Then so much the worse for change; it is an illusion. Is it impossible to think how being can be broken in pieces? Then multiplicity is an illusion. The thronging world of many things is the scene as presented by our sensibility, so patently and often so fatally misinformed. From this world of loss and frustration let us then seek the higher air, the cooler world of the spirit, the tranquil spirit, unmoving and alone, identical with the One.

From both extremes springs the hostility between appearance and reality, phenomena and noumena—there are many names for the conflict—and the consequent feud between empirical induction and explanatory deduction. The choice is offered between the surfaces of things and a problematic underlying reality. If we live in appearances then we are at their mercy; if sensibility is all, then we must pay the price. Sometimes mellow and assured— the regency villa, the thrush in the shrubbery, the yellow forsythia, the terrier sniffing round the lawn, spring on the way, all well in the morning—and then the leaden boredom of the afternoon, the sick fancies of the small hours.

But perhaps we begin by looking a gift horse in the mouth? Perhaps the duplicity we recognize in ourselves and too swiftly

see in our fellows leads us to suspect a disguise to things that is
not put on. Gerard Manley Hopkins was a Jesuit in reality and
in profession. We are not deceived by Dr Johnson's asseverations
to the contrary, he was clearly a whig of whigs. Why should
things not be what they seem to be? When we know the heat of
fire, the shock of water, the pine standing solitary on the heath,
why should we fear that the things are strange to the impressions
we have of them when our minds are open and our desires are
still? Do we not make our errors by our own fussiness and self-
seeking; are they not like clothes and emotions at second-hand,
conditions that we impose on a fresher simplicity? Perhaps, if
we let them, things will reveal themselves; if we let them, that
is if we do not try to dress them according to our taste. The
presumption should be that phenomena are revelations, not
curtains.

16. *Interlude*

Resolved to set himself to hack out an enduring shape of hard
principles and conclusions, for the soft mass of sensibility wears
to waste, he tries after breakfast as he walks up and down the
garden path. Beneath his feet he feels the soft crunch of the
damp gravel, and turning round and looking down he sees the
crescent dents of his steps behind him. His pipe is drawing well,
presently he will knock it out gently against the pear-tree bole
and the dottle will fall on the grass verge and hiss as it meets the
dew. A perfect morning. Breakfast was half-an-hour ago and he
has scanned the columns of *The Times* and noted the publication
in the *London Gazette* of the official despatches about Mediterranean operations in 1942. Before that he woke from the fervour
and irresponsibility of a dream, dissolving and lightsome and gay,
felt again the roughness of blankets and the tingle of cold water,
remembering how he was late a-bed the night before, talking,
talking, until his eyes felt gritty and the carbolic toothpaste
smarted on his oversmoked tongue.

All that is but human sensibility. What is it all about?
Images drift before his mind, half-formed thoughts and vague
drifting wants. No certain measure is composed, but there are
harmonics, and sometimes a chord, for a moment sounding
louder than the other notes, and lingering snatches of melody. He

tries to keep the consonance, but presently it dies away. Fugues do not happen, they are constructed with an effort.

Theologians tell you that you are made to the image of God, and that you are inexorably heading back to him or going out to loss; but that charity will bring you back when you are drifting away. I suppose it's all true, he reflects, I haven't the intellectual hardihood to disprove it, nor yet the energy and decision to grasp it. I suppose it's all true, yet curiously I didn't feel lost when I wasn't much of a Christian, though a part of me noted that I was technically irregular when I was out of step with most of the people who go to church, and even now, though I finished a stiff retreat two days ago and am trying to set myself to rights, isn't that just the pharisaeism of wanting the proper legal documents, of seeking protection in punctilio, of paying the insurance? Yes, I suppose it's true; then almost automatically he braces himself, yes, of course it's true. Then a murmur: but what does it matter?

What is truth anyhow and why should it matter? Of course being in tune with one's immediate environment is mellow, he muses, now when the sun in shining and the birds are singing and the retreat is behind me. But is there a truth that is more than an episode. The heart of human life, lasting and universally valid and relevant, the reality I can share with Thomas More walking in his garden at Chelsea and the thousands of my brothers and sisters who have also speculated and are now gone and long forgotten: the eyes that have looked over the yews to the line of the hills in Westmorland, and over the orange groves to the smooth bulk of Etna. All very well for the philosophers to handle the concept of truth so confidently. That's their job, like an interior decorator's having to decide whether the walls should be painted primrose or honey. All very well for the brain and for the part of me that likes to dabble in their writing, especially when they are agreeably printed and bound, and to turn to the book reviews in the *New Statesman*, the part that was arguing late last night. But what of the rest of me?

He shakes himself, and the clustering images and emotions come falling down like apples from a tree, leaving his thinking self stripped and bare, and himself feeling barren. Gunmetal twigs and branches against a grey sky, without hue or scent, without companionship or cordiality. Is winter the time for meaning?

17. *Intelligible Forms*

It has been supposed that in the many things that move about us immersed in their changing material there is an internal principle of meaning, and thus form or idea can somehow be possessed by the mind. Knowledge is a kind of communication. In knowing a tree something of the tree passes into me, not its bark and woody fibre and sap, but its form. The situation has been variously described, sometimes in story-book phrases, sometimes by mechanical models, sometimes in terms more learned and difficult to grasp; the supposition generally is that there is a duplication of the tree in my perception.

Here am I; there is a tree: how do both mingle in my act of knowledge? Perhaps a kind of little tree has sprouted in my mind? —the suggestion is not so crude as it sounds, for the possibility has been entertained by some philosophers who have worked their way through the problem of knowledge only to end up with some such explanation. Or is there a prolongation of the tree from the garden into me, a mysterious streaming out of energy, an effluence of atoms or images as Democritus thought, rays and particles, trickier and more variable but ultimately as physical as those that cause changes in a photographic plate. Here again a doctrine as old as the Greeks has been revived by modern physiological philosophers.

It was a Greek, too, who put forward a subtler solution which allows for the special characteristics of knowledge. Here is a transformation different from all physical processes because the subject knowing takes the object known without appearing to change it or to suffer a physical change himself. Now most natural actions and reactions conform to the type of eating and drinking, even the purely biological functions of sex can be set in the same category. The impulse is to avoid death, to absorb, to expand; the result is to destroy something else, until in the end something else destroys you. 'Getting and spending, we lay waste our powers.' Our environment is our food, ultimately we are its food. So the tide of action ebbs and flows; the cycle of birth and death; the generation of one thing the corruption of another.

One is agent and the other is patient and a real change is induced by their connection. But set above this growth and decay there is a special kind of motion, biologically based but not biologically enclosed, springing from the source of life, but not wholly carried along by the stream and immersed. Modest and almost furtive in its lowest manifestations, proud and assured in its highest, there is a motion that brings no death, a laying hold that is not a predatory, a possession without aggrandisement, an embrace that preserves a distance, a challenge to mortality.

Running it never runs from us away.

Here is the operation of knowing; a promise for those born twice, a doom for those who may find the second death. But we are running too fast ahead, and may not yet speak of its fullness.

When I know a tree I remain myself, and the tree remains intact. This would not be the case were I to attempt to eat the tree, or beat on the tree; one of us, or both, would suffer. It was Aristotle who insisted that in knowing there was a special kind of interchange that was not physical change and could not be reduced to material transformation. What a tremendous exception enters so unobtrusively into the field of the *Physics*. In the world of nature, not to speak of the world of grace, everything is not either eater or eaten. Anticipated and rejected was Feuerbach's dictum that man is what he eats. In knowledge there is a breath of *pneuma*, an undecaying activity, a spiritual stirring that cannot be reduced to the load of matter and the crumbling and corruption of bodies. The scholastic contrast this *immutatio spiritualis* with the *immutatio materialis*; knower and known somehow—*quoddammodo* they say—share a common form, yet without physical fusion of their distinct identities. This is the anthem of *The Phoenix and the Turtle:*—

> So they loved, as love in twain
> Had the essence but in one;
> Two distincts, division none;
> Number there in love was slain . . .
>
> Distance, and no space was seen . . .

> Property was thus appalled,
> That the self was not the same;
> Single nature's double name
> Neither two nor one was called.
>
> Reason in itself confounded,
> Saw division grow together,
> To themselves yet either neigher,
> Simple were so well compounded.

And it sounds through the metaphysical poets.

> Where can we finde two better Hemispheres
> Without sharpe North, without declining West?

The problem of knowledge rises from our enquiry into the nature and content of the form shared by knower and known. The occasion is not merely academic, for we perform the transformation at every waking moment of our truly human living, nor can we reflect on it without emotion, for the tree in the mind seems to be a tree without sap, and the tree in the ground and unknown seems to make no sense.

18. *Representations*

Although ideas may be, as Aristotle says, likenesses of things, or natural signs expressing their object as spontaneously as cries of joy or moans of pain, not conventional ciphers in arbitrary relation to their objects, as the words of language are to things, nevertheless once they are described as delegates they soon become intermediaries and then, almost imperceptibly, substitutes. St Thomas himself says that a thing in the mind is better than a thing in nature—the point of the comparison may be admitted, the necessity regretted.

Inner representations of outer things are postulated in sensation and intellection alike. But whereas the forms of sensation are supposed to be impressed on the senses by phenomena or sensible objects, the forms of intellection, namely the meanings of things, are supposed to derive at least partially from the reason itself: most philosophers, including many realists, agree that the objects of our experience are unable of themselves to manifest a meaning. Particular facts are doggedly themselves and nothing else until the reason gets to work on them: they are but a chance heap of events until they are interpreted into a pattern; they are like the unrelated figures that dance before the eyes when you have been doing the accounts and are too tired to tot up the columns. It is the reason that takes a sensible object and elaborates it into an idea; from that doctrine the transition is not difficult to the doctrine that the reason makes it up.

> The mind, that ocean, where each kind
> Does straight its own resemblance find;
> Yet it creates, transcending these,
> Far other worlds, and other seas.

The problem lies over these far other worlds and other seas.

We make trouble for ourselves when we treat the mental form or idea as though it were in itself the first object of knowledge, whereas its formal content is not a thing, but a relation to a thing. Of all the categories of reality relations are the most baffling to the reflective reason, which tends to isolate its object of study and treat it, anyhow for the period, as a kind of absolute or thing in itself. Moreover the accompanying play of imagination usually tends to solidify the terms. Only if the meaning of a relation is with an effort kept fluid and entirely beckoning out of itself shall we be able to appreciate how through a mental form, a relation of a thing to a thing rather than a thing itself, the knower is made like the known, and only so can the mental assimilation be explained without postulating a little idol or facsimile.

Whereas most of the ancient and medieval philosophers were not preoccupied with mental forms, more recent philosophers have been tempted to pause over them and have found it difficult to move on. For once the inner representation is taken as the first object of direct knowledge the problem of knowledge has been insinuated. How do we know that the idea of a thing corresponds with the thing itself? It may be helpful to watch now how the plot proceeds to thicken.

The mental form or representation was introduced in the first place to explain how an object in reality outside me can be brought within me and yet remain unchanged. We can neglect for the present the various attempts that have been made to explain the production of this representation; they are the topic more for the psychologist than for the epistemologist. For instance the controversy between platonists and aristoteleans as to whether our ideas are innate or acquired does not directly affect the realism of the knowledge that results. The epistemological problem is about the content, not the origin, of knowledge. Though St Thomas sides with the aristotalians he sees no inherent impossibility in the views of the platonists; both schools alike have to face the same problem of knowledge, and both, whatever their doctrines about its origin, have sometimes ended in the position of saying that the representation of a tree gives me truthful knowledge when it is a faithful copy, either of a heavenly or of an earthly tree as the case may be.

Already the problem is running on the wrong lines, which will prove in the event to be a siding to the buffers of doubt out of which the mind can escape only by backing. But we anticipate. The conclusion is tantamount to the admission that what is known directly and immediately is a substitute-tree, with but this proviso, that it tallies with the real tree.

Yet what is the test of correspondence? We speak of the severely rational test, for no doubt there are others, the test of confident living, of adjustment to environment and so forth. From the psychological point of view, both as regards the individual and the group, it seems healthier to be certain in a superstition than bewildered in a doubt. It will be generally allowed that realism scores on the pragmatic tests, and that the practical reason must set itself to act for ends about the existence and nature of which the theoretical reason has no assurance. But where is the theoretical guarantee that ideas correspond with things? The guarantees we would apply, are not they themselves ideas?

A usual reply is to the effect that something must cause our ideas; the piston drives only from a pressure, the mind must be filled before it can think, and therefore there is a principle other than the thinking subject. But that will not do, for the principle of causality is itself a mental judgement composed of ideas. How do we know that it corresponds with a non-mental reality, how can we use it to reach out and be reassured when, for all we know, causality, though perhaps a strict law of thought, may not at all apply to extra-mental reality, if indeed such exists? To attempt to prove reality through causality seems therefore to fall into the fallacy of the vicious circle.

Psychologically speaking there is of course a great difference between an object we see and an object we have seen and now recall and an object we make up for ourselves. In one case we have the sentiment of being acted on, in another the sentiment of reproducing from within what has acted on us in the past, in the third case we have the sentiment of inventing our own world. Between the first and the second there is the difference of the outward and the inward eye—as in Wordsworth's poem on the daffodils—but the third opens out into the world of make-believe which we know to be such. These psychological data are impressive in their own order and may provide the psychologist with his tests for living in the real world or in a dream world. But though he may judge mental states as responses and adaptations to an environment, he cannot himself prove the existence of that environment.

So long as ideas are taken as the first terms of knowledge and while rational consciousness reflects on that supposition, the more the mind buzzes like a bluebottle on the window pane, shut in and unable to fly out into the open air. Or rather, imagine that, instead of transparent glass, the mind is against a mirror, with the realists saying that the images are cast on the mirror from elsewhere and the idealists saying that since the mirror is a mental mirror we cannot say that its images are anything else but mental. In any case, as Logan Pearsall Smith says, all mirrors are magical mirrors: we can never see our real faces. So may we picture the dispute between two schools in philosophy that lasted for nearly two hundred years beginning with the seventeenth century, a dispute won by the mentalists so long as purely rational evidence was appealed to and by their opponents when other influences were allowed. Both sides however agreed that the first object of thought was a mental state.

For purposes of debate, both sides assumed as a setting the existence of two parallel orders, the world of thought and the world of non-mental things. You were a realist if you held that clear and careful thoughts matched things and that your mental plans could be shown to correspond to the world outside. The mind was stored with pictures, the main effort of criticism was to discern between the true copies and the distortions, and this could be done by tidying the mind and eliminating the murkier elements of passion and superstition and by directing what was left to the discovery and control of the material world. At the outset this taste for clear ideas and mechanical experiment produced a great advance of knowledge, and though its principles came to be doubted they have remained as working postulates for most of the later expansions of science.

In the realm of purely philosophic criticism, however, the realists fought a losing battle in their attempt to establish the correspondence between mind and object. For once the first object of mind is set up as something within the mind we have shut ourselves in: we may escape as engineers or even as men of feeling, but as philosophers we are occupied with mental states, which presently become notions, and these presently become ciphers; from playing with thoughts we come to amuse ourselves with words, and then finally fall into an agnostic silence. The trouble sets in with the first idolatry of thought: in how many ways is man better than the idols he makes.

19. *Indirect Realism*

The theory that ideas are immediate objects of perception and that these are copies of an external reality is probably what most people would profess if they were asked to show a reason for their ordinary and naive realism. When I see something there is a photographic image on my retina, and when it rustles there is a corresponding impression on the tympanum of my ear, and from these and many other effects the mind builds up a concept or idea. This is supposed to be the first and direct object of my rational knowledge, conformable to outside reality when it has passed the current tests that discriminate between common and sober perceptions on one hand and bizarreries and hallucination on the other. Thus we can be said to know what lies outside us.

> As yet by books and swains the world he knew,
> Nor knew if books and swains report it true.

Philosophical analysis, however, did not report it true. The conceptualization of knowledge was presently attended by a disintegrating criticism. First of all there was the separation of sensibility from the hard and fast properties of outside things. Our perception of qualities was loosened from external reality when they were taken to be highly personal glosses arising from a merely mechanical interaction of two things. Physiologically an excitation of the optic nerve produces what is commonly called the sensation of light, and this might come about either at the aspect of the thing when the eye was open or from pressure on the eye-ball when the lid was closed. It was observed psychologically that we select and interpret the elements of the situation: grey seems pink on green and green on pink, yet physically it remains the same piece of grey paper whatever the background. Our sensations and judgements about other qualities were considered to suffer from a similar subjectivism and though, no doubt, it was important and valuable, particularly for purposes of psychological assessment, to study personal reactions and imagined sensibility as acutely as possible, the only strictly scientific security lay in getting down to what was impersonally measurable.

At first the growing power and fashion of the mathematically physical sciences made this acceptable. It was assumed that the scientist could dispense with the secondary qualities and feel the easier for so doing. They could be left as modalities of our mind, while the real scientist got down to work on the primary characteristics of the world, on what was solid and measurable. From the concepts of movement, mass, space, and time the edifice of science could be constructed. We could afford to neglect qualities when they could not be transposed into quantitative terms, which alone were safe and secure like hard cash.

Qualities were all very well for the poets, or for our off moments of pensiveness; but quantity, ah that was the stuff. Nevertheless the mind was to find no security there after all, for quantity was to prove very thin ice, unable to bear the weight of theory laid on it. For were not space and time themselves mental categories? They were what the mind read into its mysterious environment, patterns imposed to tidy up what is ultimately chaotic and unknowable. The very particles of quantity themselves were presently to dissolve into fundamentally unpredictable centres of energy, so that the whole quantitative scheme eventually came to be seen, not as a framework in which we are lodged, but as a set of approximate rules we make to codify some statistical frequencies in our consciousness.

These patterns are what we know, and the mind spins them, for all we can tell, from its own resources, like a spider spinning a web from its own belly. That there is an answering reality is a truth we cannot theoretically establish, though we may be practicably certain about it perhaps on moral grounds, for whatever the pure reason may say we may yet have a lively religious confidence that a benevolent providence would not allow us to be deceived. Hence we may rule out the possibility that we are born distorted and therefore distort everything we see and lay the ghost of a malevolent world-spirit who contrives that all our perceptions are illusory. The theoretic reason, however, roused from its dogmatic slumbers, cannot escape its fate and is doomed to wander homeless like the Flying Dutchman. There are no proper guarantees that ideas match a non-mental reality. We know representations, but representations of what? There is the boundary, the limit of our knowledge.

All this follows from the initial assumption that what I know is my state of mind. A thing outside my consciousness could be known only by inference, and this process, when it would pass from a conceptual meaning to an existential fact, is of suspect validity. The object is within my consciousness: to attempt to conceive it without this relationship is either to credit it with another relationship to mind, which does not help the realist, or make it inconceivable, for we should be imputing meaning to what for us has no meaning at all. Hence we can have no idea of what *is* apart from the *is* in consciousness: being is being conceived. We are landed into what has been called the Egocentric Predicament.

When we think of our world as a system of related terms we are proceeding to lock ourselves in even more effectively. The relations which penetrate and modify the terms are imposed by the synthetic activity of the mind. The subject knowing changes the object known. Were the object unchanged and independent of our mind it would be unknown by our mind. Again the same dilemma confronts us, either we do not conceive a non-mental reality, in which case it might possibly exist, on condition we did not permit ourselves to think it, or we conceive what we think is a non-mental reality and by that very fact we make it mental. But, as not infrequently, the dilemma is not so intimidating as it has been made out to be. Relations are in a peculiar category of reality; unlike other real modes they do not add a real entity to their subjects.

20. Some Consequences

If all thinking is reputed to be of mental stuff through and through and nothing else is digestible, idealism can wax bolder and more radical, as in fact it did. Why postulate an unknown x outside the mind? Why try to throw out a bridge of which the arch will remain unfinished and in the air? Surely truth is not a problematic attachment to the material world but is expressed in purely ideal coherences, and perhaps comes from the conformity of my fugitive reflections with a greater and more absolute mind in which my own consciousness is somehow caught up. Yet there are difficulties here, and many contrary interpretations. According to some it is doubtful whether such a World-Mind can be reached from the mental necessities the reasoning reason finds indispensable for the conduct of its scientific processes. Individual consciousness anyhow is revealed in a sense of separation, and my identity with a transcendental mind can lie only in unconsciousness. Hence the tendency to dissolve the edges of thought, hence possibly the cult of personal extinction. The course of ideas was matched by the fashion in landscape; the clearness of Canaletto, duskier in Guardi, melted into the impressionism of Turner. The problem of knowledge could be lost by sinking personal consciousness and merging ourselves into our unmindful surroundings. We may be swallowed up, but the alternative is to be content with dry and pattering noises inside, like a bird in a cage.

So the dislocation in the premises proceeds fatally to its conclusion. No other escape is possible once the mind is shut up with ideas instead of things, even though the intention had been to re-discover reality eventually. Unable to feed on nature the mind will come to chew on itself. It may survive temporarily on its own interior resources, but logic is only roughage and no sort of nourishment, and eventually even the rules of coherence may fade away. Unless the mind be born again, through the acceptance of a reality other and greater than itself, it will linger in its prison, wavering in the consciousness of its own responses without settled convictions that they belong to a fuller world of purposes. The problem has a parallel in the moral order, where a sense of guilt turns morbid when no expression and means of expiation can be found.

The issue was not immediately tragic except to those integral characters who tried to live as they thought. Some found the tragic solitude intolerable and threw it off by death; others shuffled it off and sought relief in the cults of appetite, instinct, and custom. Most men, however, can manage to live with an unresolved speculative doubt; professional philosophers kept their theoretical reason in a compartment, and so were able to keep their jobs and their wives and die full of German academic honours and not too poorly off. Though we may criticize them, as Thackeray did Byron, for not writing from his heart—'filling high a cup of Samian wine' in words but preferring to drink gin-and-water in fact—historical appreciation can make the criticism seem trivial when it sets them in the nineteenth-century picture of romantic agnosticism. They brooded over one another's books and contributions to learned periodicals, whatever the inner doubt there was no parsimony of words or lack of sounding phrases, and whatever the inner congestion of strange and transcendental terms there was a great deal of outward prosperity. As they sat at their ornate and varnished pine desks in their studies, papered in sombre Venetian-red and stuffy from the glossy stove, they could see their neighbour's new villa of undressed stone going up in the Rhine baronial style, the pine woods beyond where they could walk in droves and sing their songs, in major keys and two-four time about wine and in minor keys and three-four time about maidens dropping to a decline; the feather of smoke down the valley was the railway train bringing the punctual mail and promising the way to Italy; the needle gun had been invented, culture was expanding like the heavy industries in Silesia and the Ruhr; and they had all the confidence of a nation that needed to affirm its prosperity and superiority.

Another divorce had been made, and it seemed to be working very well. Two centuries before philosophy had separated from letters, and now science had separated from philosophy. Theory

and practice drew apart and went their separate ways, in some cases
within the same personality. A working scientist was too busy
and successful to worry himself with transcendental vapours;
mechanical invention and exploitation was sufficient occupation
without theoretical anxieties. Matter was revealing more and
more secrets and in the fascination of the microscope the problem
of ultimate reality was fast receding. It was ironic that his experimental successes endowed so many metaphysicals with the
funds and leisure to buzz more and more sonorously in a vacancy:
of course they were esteemed characters, but except for those who
furthered political ends in building up the monstrous theory of
the German State, they were not expected to be immediately
relevant.

The science of the period that remained closest to philosophy
was psychology. Before it was captured by mechanism and turned
into a superior department of physiology, psychology had been
taken to mean study of consciousness, an internal state whose data
were to be observed by looking within. The cleavage between
inside and *outside* was accepted. You could choose between the
tenuous dreaminess of the one or the brisk practicalities of the
other. In Scotland and France, however, a tradition of experimental philosophy lingered on, a humane positivism was more
congenial than transcendentalism; their people were certainly
practical, and not without intellectual hardihood, nor were they
in a mood to admire the Germans; they knew the Border Ballads
in the one case and possessed a mordant humour in the other, and,
whatever the reason the academic mind in these countries was pre-
served from the more pompous and drearier forms of intellectual
agony. In England, of course, no philosophy was ever allowed to
threaten the sense of mellow earthiness and intellectual light-
heartedness.

One line of development has been roughly traced about the
problem of knowledge. Mentalism began from the later scholastics and achieved a classical though impermanent expression in
the method of Descartes. Halted by Locke it was set off again by
Berkeley and continued through the positivism of Hume.
Solemnized by Kant, though his yearnings were realist, it swelled
enormous with the later German philosophers at the turn of his
century until it clouded and darkened the land.

' "If that there King was to wake," added Tweedledum, "you'd go out—bang!—just like a candle!"

' "I shouldn't!" Alice exclaimed indignantly. "Besides, if *I'm* only a sort of thing in his dream, what are *you*, I should like to know?"

' "Ditto," said Tweedledum.

' "Ditto, ditto!" cried Tweedledee.

'He shouted this so loud that Alice couldn't help saying, "Hush! you'll be waking him, I'm afraid, if you make so much noise."

' "Well, it's no use *your* talking about waking him," said Tweedledum, "when you're only one of the things in his dream. You know very well you're not real."

' "I *am* real!" said Alice, and began to cry.

' "You won't make yourself a bit realer by crying," Tweedledee remarked: "there's nothing to cry about."

' "If I wasn't real," Alice said—half-laughing through her tears, it all seemed so ridiculous—"I shouldn't be able to cry."

' "I hope you don't suppose those are real tears?" Tweedledum interrupted in a tone of great contempt.'

CHAPTER IV

THE BREAK OUT

DOUBT is not congenial to us, for we do not easily stomach having to stand by like Tweedledee saying 'ditto, ditto.' Disillusion can be a mood of the young romantic, sombre-eyed in a garret and wearing an untidy choker, played to music which moved our great-grandparents but is now featured in the Light Programme; it can be expressed with a shrug of indifference or a whimsical humour, or with the wagging of an elderly head when it is too late to do much about it. An old man, says La Rochefoucauld, gives good advice in order to console himself for no longer being in a condition to set a bad example. But, rightly or wrongly, doubt does not last, and if it cannot be resolved by reflection then it will be broken by action.

Always there is a discomfort in man making him protest against the current assumptions of his environment, like Goya painting with pain and passion against the fluent and mannered rococo of Aranjuez. By the middle of the last century the time had come for the problem of doubt to be dissolved, if not by the tears and laughter of Alice then by other movements of feeling, by responses to powers strange to critical analysis, and by arguments with which the aristoleans and thomists, such as survived, found themselves in imperfect sympathy.

Philosophical reflection had proved a fatal danger; it was an act of Narcissus and led to his fate; and so the philosophical dogmatisms that were launched were new in their design in that they tried to cut out the speculative gear altogether. They solved the problem outside the brains-trust; they dispensed with the whole system of concepts which might or might not be adapted to an external environment; they neglected the historical debate between indirect realists and idealists, positivists and transcendentalists, as easily and confidently as an earnest believer may scrap the whole apparatus of secondary causes, such a one for instance as the Lord Londonderry who wrote of a place in his *Travels*: 'Here I learned that Almighty God, for reasons best known to himself, had been pleased to burn down my house in the county of Durham.' The new dogmatisms were like a protest of health against the sickliness of private metaphysical speculation which had gone from good to bad, from bad to worse; they resembled a man jaded by the precious art of the salons who looks afresh at the popular art of the saloons; they sought to plunge into the biological stream; and they culminated in spurt-philosophies that make no use whatever of logical analysis.

The movement of escape from philosophic doubt took many forms. The scientific materialist has already been mentioned; he is like a professional soldier who goes plodding on doing his humble duty whatever the fashions in high philosophy and policy. We are now concerned with two great movements that burst from scepticism. Their manners were contrasting, but both adopted a similar substitution of mind by will. One sought security in the demands of appetite; that is the way of the hero and his victims; one slip from him and you have the bully, another and you have the cad. The other, fearful of the social consequences of scepticism, slurred over the private and theoretic doubts of initial philosophy, and preached the dogmatism of the old and orderly traditions of society; that is the way of the statesman; one slip from him and you have the administrator, another and you have the inquisitor. Though the climate of this country has never been congenial to the extremes of either the rhapsodic or the traditionalist flourishes in philosophy, we have played with them both, and may notice them briefly in turn. 'My delight,' wrote one of our eighteenth-century countrymen, and his type happily survives, 'my delight is in the daily renewal of pleasantly interminable and happily inconclusive experiments. And have I not here,' he added, 'the very essence of all true philosophy?'

21. *The Surge*

There are two courses of knowledge, notional and real. Stretch out your hand and look at it. You form a picture of hand. But the image is detached and remote. You see the hand of a stranger. The more anxiously you look the more detached it becomes. Your representation is a double and does not really reach the hand. That is the way of knowledge that seems to have

failed us and left us with doubts. But there is another. Close your
eyes and sense your hand from within, clench your fist and feel
your fingers through pleasure and pain, playing with mud, burnt
by the flame: hand being happy, hand being hurt. Now enlarge
the sensation, know from inside what hand is loving, and hand
stained with guilt. Here, it is said, is the way of real and direct
knowledge, not through ideas and representations, but through
appetites and half-conscious motions.

Appetite may be tender in mode and noble in aspiration. In
the history of religious philosophy many movements and schools
appear which exalt affective knowledge above rational knowledge.
In fact St Thomas is the rare figure of a religious philosopher who
insists on the primacy of the intellect, though he recognizes the
limitations of the merely rational intellect and the need of a living
sympathy through love. Kant himself sought to remedy the insecurity of the pure reason with the moral obligations of the
practical reason. And no account of the reaction of appetite
against mentalism is complete without reference to the civilized
élan of Bergson and his criticism of rationalism written with great
rational humour, or to the people who have lost their way but found
their heart.

Yet we must skip the ironical to arrive at the brutal, even
though this be no more important in philosophy than Sousa is in
music. Unfortunately the protest has commanded great physical
power. This is the dogmatism that seeks to break doubt by the
protest of a powerful will; truth can be stormed by force. What
I want, that will I take. The classical stalemate is broken by a
feverish romanticism; the poise of mind upset by a display of
energy; contracts are torn up when violence will serve. The
appetite is justified by success: if there are no reasons beforehand,
the will finds them as excuses afterwards—that is the tribute the
philosophies of appetite pay to intellectualism.

This philosophy is most stridently proclaimed in the dictate
of desire, a movement of lust exaggerated into a doctrine, the
exaltation of force and inevitably the depreciation of rational
values. Apes, not brave men, drum their chests to work themselves up to the pitch. We have witnessed how weakliness of
mind and body occasions the cult of might; there is a sense of inferiority and a motion of fear when a powerful adolescent of

middle age reaches for his revolver when the word culture is uttered. But after all the masculine protest is an infantilism.

This submission to the surge has not been confined to the Nazi movement, but goes wherever there is a surrender to the play of force, whether in the blood-stream or the material forces that produce economic wealth. And with it goes a hatred of an adult civilization and of the so-called bourgeois values, for instance the idea of legislation settled by discussion and compromise, executed by men of standing with some respect for the people who cannot express themselves.

Considering the craving of human nature for safety, the reaction against rationalism is probably more dangerous, not so much when the hero behaves like a baby in a rage and a whole people follows the leader, but when people seek to sink themselves in the impersonal surge of a collective will whether embodied in the race, the proletariat, or the religious organism. We need not now attempt to appreciate the occasions and achievements of this enthusiasm; it is sufficient to see it as an attempt to descend from the stony and desolate uplands of cerebration down to the streams and moisture, which to the early Ionians, the first philosophers, was the matter of life. If thinking cannot effect this, then so much the worse for thought. Other potions will be taken so that we can mingle with the world again, even if a Dionysian frenzy is needed to interrupt the Olympian calm— 'set the feet above the brain and swear the brain is in the feet.'

The mental philosophers were displaced by the 'wild Voluntaries,' the judicious man by the genius, seizing systems and slighting rules. The romantic movement was in full swing. But presently it was succeeded by a wave of pessimism, and then it was no longer a matter of a taste for gothic novels in a regency drawing room, and certainly nothing so healthy and full of zest as the Byronic legend, but the search for the dark and secret streams that flow over the edge into waste and destruction.

22. The Cumeelfoh

The philosopher, thought Plato, is like a man in a den of wild beasts: he was paying a doubtful compliment, nevertheless a movement of philosophy, whatever its first extravagance, tends to settle down into a code. Though the history of voluntarism can illustrate the truth of Pope's line

the worst of madmen is a Saint run mad

there were, and especially in England, many examples of philosophers who combined their speculations with a responsible sense of public decorum. Contemporary with the shagginess and heroic barbarism we have been describing, and similar, not certainly in its randiness but in its revulsion from the transcendental intellectualists, a politer and socially more influential motion of impatience with the problems of scepticism may be noticed. It had already started as a reaction against the rationalism of the Enlightenment and the French Revolution.

This was the dogmatism of good custom, which appealed from the criticisms of the pure reason to the traditions of a going concern: intellectual brilliance had to be placed in the setting of political good sense; the spirit of Greek speculation tempered by the laws of Roman order. It may seem farcical to claim a resemblance, yet the social consciousness of Jane Austen and of Lamartine were equally alien to a metaphysical criticism of knowledge, and both knew that you cannot disregard what the world says.

British scepticism had usually accompanied a cool and genteel attitude, and offered no hindrance to good estate management, the duties of a churchwarden, and the efficient execution of affairs of State. English philosophers, someone has remarked, always give the impression of being well-laundered. And so characteristically from the policies of the lowland gentry who were then beginning to consolidate the British Empire, building their Adam houses on the spoils of India and looking a trifle bleakly at enthusiasm, came the appeal to commonsense. They found sublimity in strokes by Dr Akenside and Dr Beattie and in the newly discovered taste for scenery. Their sublimity became the picturesque, and they liked to have it framed. They jingled the guineas in their breeches-pockets and gazed with admiration on the compositions of Claude. 'An old tower in the middle of a deep wood,' says the Reverend Dr Archibald Alison, 'a bridge slung across a chasm between rocks, a cottage on a precipice.' There was always a bridge. The spirit was shrewd yet complacent, unaspiring yet not ignoble.

Though this sobriety was reflected on the continent in the sentiment of the governing classes in the reign of Louis-Phillipe, the appeal to tradition was generally speaking rather more strained and solemn. In this country the solidarity of most voters with the community was more assured, if less articulate. The country gentry and the Liverpool and Glasgow merchants understood one another pretty well, and even the mechanics for the most part shared the thoughts of the masters and owners. We had never enthroned the Goddess of Reason on a high altar nor had we suffered the humiliation of Jena. We had controlled a small revolution of our own in the grand manner a century-and-a-half before, an affair of oligarchs that had been successfully covered with popular glory, and now having pulled down the Corsican, we were secure in our impregnable myth, the Whig Interpretation of History. We could appeal to Magna Charta and a burly Protestantism and a contempt for foreign ways, and succeed with a unanimity denied more regimented peoples. Perhaps it was because we were on the make and doing well, but we found no need to invoke our ancestors with a solemnity quite equal to that of the Traditionalists on the Continent, and anyhow we were spared the Bourbons. Burke's oratory had expounded the philosophy to the members of Parliament fifty years before, though he was then, as Goldsmith wrote,

Too deep for his hearers, still went on refining,
And thought of convincing, while they thought of dining.

It was not until after the rise of the Oxford movement and Oriental Studies and the abolition of the East India Company and after men of other cultures entered our public and academic life that we began to lose our self-sufficiency and confidence.

Abroad the appeal had to be made across the chasm of the Revolution. It was sounded in many tones; of regret for a vanished chivalry, wistfulness for a rural philosophy, apostrophes to the wedding of Teutonic energy and Mediterranean order, invocations of a *Volkgeist*, repetitions of the mass of convictions produced by the interactions of immemorial institutions and human nature on one another. It was present in the writings of de Bonald, in the Gothic restorations of Viollet-le-Duc and Romanesque reconstructions of Abadie and, less temperately, in the eloquence of Donoso Cortes and the dreams of mad Ludwig. Conservatism had found a philosophy the old Duke of Wellington would not have recognized, a philosophy that was rather like Mr George Jones the painter, who complained that he was embarrassed because he was frequently mistaken for the victor of Waterloo: 'That's a damned odd thing, Jones,' remarked the old man after a pause, 'for nobody has mistaken me for you.'

The wisdom of the ages was thought to supply for the inherent impotence of personal speculation, the voice of God transmitted through tradition for the conflicting doctrines of the philosophical sects. The Pope of Rome was proposed as the most august representative of tradition, even by people who were not notably ultramontane in their other beliefs. One can say of Europe, says de Maistre, what Gibbon said of France: this realm has been made by bishops. The Pope was to be the mouthpiece of the new movement according to one of the greatest of the traditionalists whose journal by a paradox was called *L'Avenir*; but the Pontiff was not sensitive to the honour and lost the confidence of Lamennais, who turned instead to the wisdom he was optimistic enough to think could spring from universal suffrage.

But were our ancestors wiser than we? Perhaps not, the argument runs, but, after allowing for the tendency to see the past bathed in a sunset glow, it may be contended that they seemed to be more confident. If they did not practise them, nevertheless they seemed surer about what were the elemental decencies. Historical research has done something to mitigate that judgement, and at the time it was enquired how our forefathers, who lacked traditions, came to be right. The Christian could answer with the doctrine of a primitive revelation, and this was not unconfirmed by the findings of contemporary studies in comparative religion.

Many of the contemporary arguments used by Traditionalism now seem to be special pleading, but apart from its failure to appreciate the social function of personal rational integrity—

> They are slaves who fail to be
> In the right with two or three

—the movement was a sound attempt to recapture an original community confidence, a reaction against the disintegrating criticism of a few analytically disposed individuals and to tap again a corporate consciousness, a thinking together, operative before any attempt to rationalize it, a solidarity of men with nature and of men with men older than philosophy. Yet the times were not propitious, for the peasants were not conspicuous for their public spirit, the artisans were the new rootless proletariat, the industrialists were in the competition for private profits, and the representatives of the ancient aristocracy were not strong enough to bear the burden of the past. It was difficult to sing seriously with Lord John Manners:

> Let wealth and commerce, laws and learning die,
> But leave us still our old nobility.

In any case, no class has a vested interest in truth, certainly not a propertied class. *Les Soirées de Saint-Petersbourg* was to precede a blood-red dawn. But if the lay representatives of the old culture could not meet the occasion, there was still the support of the ancient religion.

23. *Religion and Action*

Quid revolvis? Tertullian had cried, *Deus praecipit.* Why debate? God commands. It seemed to many citizens in the last century that the last resource against philosophic doubt is found in religious faith. Such fideism, the doctrine that devotional belief can supply what is wanting in the proper activity of the reason and can operate without the need of rational reassurance, has not been confined to any one period and is endemic wherever religion lays claim to being more than a mildly ethical code, but in the nineteenth century it was argued with great journalistic skill and naturally not without approval from some of the representatives of organized religion.

The reason was blackguarded for leading us to the waste land, and the longer we continued with it the more threatening would be our lot. 'My reason,' Montaigne had said, 'is not framed to bend or stoop; my knees are.' The principles were the same, the conclusion different. We were counselled to make the leap of faith and set doubts behind us. If we live according to the heart the trap will be broken and we shall be liberated, religion needs no recommendation from or to the reason; on the contrary, the more

flagrant the affronts it offers to the academics the more attractive
it will appear to men of spirit. Hume rather sourly speaks of 'the
usual propensity of mankind towards the marvellous,' but it seems
that the more shocking and frequent the miracles and portents
that accompany religion the more it appeals even to those not
naturally credulous. The play of human life teases the too sober
methods of scientific investigation; there is a humour in the work-
ings of providence, and it must be confessed that many religious
men are not very sensitive about scandalizing the scientists. The
fascination of unreason to the reasoning, as of tales of violence to
men of peace, deserves a special study.

But for Catholics, who are commonly taken as the classical
exponents of how to use faith as a substitute for reason, the story
ends when, under the presidency of a pope widely regarded as a
typical obscurantist, the Vatican Council emphatically rejected
this dubious despotism of faith and, more majestically than in any
pronouncement of the Age of Reason, defended the rights of the
reason to discuss the existence and nature of God. *Quid Athenae
Hierosolymis?*—Tertullian's rhetorical question was answered, but
not in his sense.

The strongly reasonable central tradition of Latin Christianity
is very old, and knows that, as the Trimmer wrote, 'tho' in some
dearly beloved audience *Good Resolute Nonsense* backed with
Authority may prevail . . . now the world is grown saucie and
expecteth Reasons, and good ones too.' It has certainly not been
an enclave for philosophers and many strange and fantastic events
have attended its progress, and these of course have been written
up at length. But to the classical doctrine they are so many preliminary flourishes and gestures of high spirits rather than motions
to or from the heart of the matter. And though official christianity has not lacked a shrewd and opportunist spirit in political
matters nor a sound administrative temper in the conduct of
affairs, it has generally exhibited a strong disinclination to regard
its dogmas and morals as a social service.

Despite canvassing, extremist views have not engaged the
profound interest of the English; their inmost convictions are
touched with a quizzical sobriety and influenced by what is demanded for the benefit of the whole. They have never been a
subject people. Thought is strongly ethical and filled with regard

for what is owing to the community—or to the convention; it is dominated with what will prove useful and what will do good. The moral imperative is social, and strictly practicable. So although a man may play about with doubts as to the foundations of pure thinking he does not thereby lose his sense of security: there is a spirit of a game about such thinking; but it is not frivolous. There is no heartfelt distrust of the force of certain general affirmations of duty and decency, and of the consequences and exigences of reality that cannot be neglected without imperilling social life.

All this is held instinctively rather than articulately demonstrated. It is felt that this sort of realism has no need of proof; it is its own natural and unapologetic justification, it fits in with the facts and accords with the kindlier scientific temper of the age. Why seek metaphysical explanations when such an attitude is fortified by the solid success of the sciences? We may chase our theoretical doubts round and round in circles if we choose, but we are here to build. Idealism is a practical impossibility, but realism works. Results are more important than processes, and most of us feel sympathy with the broker's clerk in South Africa; 'Efforts are being made,' says the correspondent of *The Times* newspaper, 'to enable the young man, who is one of a family of eight, to go to the university. When at school his marks for mathematics were never high, because, although his answers were always right, his method of solving problems was always either unexplained or unorthodox.'

24. Pragmatism

Our answers may be right, but the reasons may be unexplained or unorthodox. They are retrospective, and insufficient at that. This reflection has been developed by a general philosophy based on a psychological analysis of human action rather than on an appeal to the tenets of religion taken in a confessional sense or to the conventions of a culture taken in a provincial sense. The human reason has the paradoxical power of attacking itself by using its own instruments. The sceptics are saltier than the dogmatists and the rhapsodic school of philosophy on occasion can command an excellent style of expository prose. Attending donnishness is the temptation to be anti-academic and anti-rational;

there is a similar tendency among clergymen to be heartily worldly and broadminded. Certainly the movement of impatience with the reasoning reason does not lack trained philosophical support.

What should be the purpose of thought? Action. What is the purpose of action? Happiness. What in fact is the result of philosophical criticism? Inaction. Fortunately we are not disembodied critical intelligences. There is within us a biological urge or a lyrical instinct, call it what you will, that carries us beyond the merely rational evidence of a situation. Thought—action—success: that is the perfect order released in a developing series, whose successive alternations always leave the non-rational elements in stronger and more secure possession. Even science is really the sort of magic that works.

I conceive something, I act according to it, and in the event I am better adapted to my environment. Anyhow I advance. Or perhaps I find myself acting and then make the best of it: we need not settle here whether in the first place concept comes before action or contrariwise. Then I evoke another and perhaps conflicting conception and act accordingly, and again I advance. I may make mistakes, but by and large it seems possible to run a fairly successful life that is not patient of purely rational analysis. Is not this the method of the experimental sciences and the biographical pattern of individual achievement? Wise men are trimmers in the best sense of the word, readjusting themselves to every change of environment, refusing to become set in their ways, remaining supple and responsive.

To ask whether one fixed judgement can be true to things as they are is a false question unless it is related to what happens when it is adopted. Certain principles have been found to work and to be beneficial; they may be called true, in the sense that they are verified in practice. If God did not exist it would be necessary to invent him. We have to pretend that things are true, that we are free, that men are brothers, and that virtue either is its own reward or pays in the long run. Do not bridle if you are called a pragmatist, or be rattled if a debater forces you into the position of admitting that there is neither true nor false, but only successful and unsuccessful. Confess to a hearty respect for success, not the success dangled before us by the correspondence business schools nor the *réclame* of the go-getter, but the achievement that

will meet with the approval of most people you like and respect.
Act at all costs. Make up your mind, the turn of the event will
tell you whether you were right; there is no other test for what is
good, and truth is the recognition of what is good; even the old
scholastics could not improve on the definition that good is what
we like and what makes us happy when we have it. The step is
taken, and rationalized afterwards. 'If you have the decision,'
said a judge, 'reasons will be found to be as plentiful as black-
berries.'

Theoretic ideas therefore slip into second place, and since the
problem of knowledge is entirely in the world of theory we can
treat it like veterans spinning a yarn about their past campaigns.
The issue has already been settled in favour of realism, nevertheless it is interesting to discuss what might have been had things
been otherwise. We think that ideas are operative, but this is
only by courtesy when they fit in with what we do. 'Let me give
you an illustration,' says St Clement of Alexandria, 'you ought to
doubt whether it is right for a man to get drunk; but your practice
is to get drunk before considering the question.'

Now there is much to be said in favour of pragmatism. It is
genial to start with; 'to cut with a sharp knife a bright green
water-melon on a big scarlet plate of a summer afternoon. Ah,
is not this happiness!' Then a deep vein of realism runs through
the assumption that if we act according to our wants we shall both
find ourselves and fit in with a greater whole; it stresses the
sterility of merely rational criticism and recognizes what has been
confirmed by a century of mentalism, namely, that the human
reason unless supported from resources outside itself falls back
exhausted from the systems it constructs, like the Portuguese after
their vast explorations and colonization of the sixteenth century.

There is also much to be said against pragmatism, chiefly
because it does not push psychological analysis far enough. A
course of action is substituted for an insight into reasons and
preaches prudence without ends. It claims to be a theory and
therefore defeats itself. Pragmatism rationalized ceases to be
itself. It incurs the criticisms Plato directed against hedonism,
of mistaking a consequent for a constituent and of thinking that
the statement that things are good when they give us pleasure
exempts us from enquiring why they give us pleasure: similarly

pragmatism may put the cart before the horse in putting practical success before theoretical truth. It is subject also to the criticisms directed against fideism, without the credit of a gallant venture; the tragic nobility of the reason is not respected, for many would rather know the truth even though it made them unhappy and insecure, and more in their heart of hearts would not think of measuring their actions by the event. The English enjoy a reputation for pragmatism, yet no other people entertain such a veneration for the losing battles they have fought, perhaps because none was final—Corunna, Balaclava, Mons, Dardanelles, Dunkirk, Arnhem, those are the names we celebrate. Nor, may one add, do other people manifest the same affection for their victorious opponents—Joan of Arc, Saxe, Washington, Ney, Rommel.

Furthermore pragmatism seems to fail by its own test, for it does not work. The men who have professed it have been better than their theory. While a good negative test of truth is offered, anything that is hopelessly strained and unworkable can be judged to suffer from such inherent defect that neither the positive criterion of truth nor even the decisive guide to action is supplied. The prospect of success is not man's stimulus, for he is happy only on condition he thinks an absolute standard has been found, which calls forth his full service and against which he can square himself. He is not really content when he measures the world by himself. He wants to be right, rather than to be gratified. He is not so constituted that he can be happy with a working hypothesis; rightly or wrongly he seeks to know what is. It is not enough to be retrospective and to know how things have come to be and how he has come to arrive at what he holds, to tolerate the material causes and assign what may be an efficient cause; he would penetrate into what things are, and we among them, their content, meaning, idea, and formal causes. Underneath their tonic cynicism and geniality, the pragmatists themselves bear witness to a passion for truth for its own sake. They show what a second-best is the hypothesis *as if* compared to the contemplation of *is*.

CHAPTER V

THE LOADED MIND

IF dogmatism be examined, and especially the dogmatism appealing to good sense, tradition, and common consent, it will be found to repose on the conviction that there are truths above criticism, commonplaces implicit in all affirmations, denials, and discussions. They include the first principles of thought, and the sentiment that the self exists and that the mind has a bent towards and a need for an object other than itself.

On analysis such assumptions will be found to transcend commonsense. Their consequences are currently accepted, for they are conditions of reasonableness, yet their central truth is beyond the reach of experiment and experience, and can be inwardly scrutinized, if at all, only by the speculative and curious naked intellect. Agree to the judgement that being is being, and you are at once caught up in metaphysics, for you are saying what may indeed be prompted, yet not uttered by the ordinary experience of fact. Moreover that I exist, not merely as an historical incident nor as a contingent kink in an atomic trajectory, but as a thing, able to make enunciations possessing eternal and universal validity; furthermore, that I am made for the sheer truth and for nothing less, not for temporary accommodations to my shifting and passing away environment—these are statements lifted far above the reach of commonsense alone.

To commonsense they are postulates. But a postulate is an arbitrary premiss accepted for the purpose of a limited enquiry and discussion. It belongs to a special and particular science and has little place in a general science that leaves nothing outside its field. This must be based, not on an act of faith, but on an understanding of its principles. An unreflective positivism is all very well so far as it goes. But since its special premisses appear to be doubted by some thinkers, it will be well to widen the enquiry and, taking their philosophism on its own ground, see if we can there defend a realist position.

25. *Useful Doubt*

Remembering what happened to the room swept and garnished, warned that the emptied mind in philosophy can be as dangerous as the emptied heart in the life of devotion, nevertheless let us begin in a spirit of detachment. St Thomas calls it a *universalis dubitatio de veritate*, a weighing up of presuppositions; an attitude that is neither a make believe to see what happens when everything is questioned nor yet a paralyzing inactivity; but a genuine hesitation, a pause to see if an intellectual way of escaping out of mentalism appears.

Doubt is a state of mind, not an act of mind. There are two kinds of doubt; one lies in blank ignorance, as when I hesitate between two opposites because I know nothing whatever about either of them; the other lies in the knowledge of the balance of seemingly equal reasons for opposites. The former is called negative doubt, and while no blame may attach to it, there is certainly no usefulness to be expected from it: it is the absence of thought, inert and unproductive. Since our minds must work in one way or the other, and since we presume that the problems of philosophy are worth tackling, it is not the kind of doubt we can adopt here. But the latter, which is called positive doubt, is different: it is tension and perhaps an expectation, a poise, we hope, preceding a spring.

Now whether a state of real and positive doubt is feasible when the mind is first confronted with its object is not at all certain. That we can entertain positive doubts on special points of detail is obvious, also that we can withhold assent from our normal convictions during periods in which we choose to look at the arguments against them. There is evidence on both sides, and we can allow ourselves to be influenced by one side or the other. This is notably apparent with regard to the conclusions we hold by inference: a theist may be convinced by the rigour of his demonstrations for the existence of God, and yet his mind can admit the difficulties against his position: a believer can suffer an agony denied the unbeliever. Any derivative truth can be held in suspense, and since we are usually dealing with inferences, even when we are working towards the very foundations of thought, it is not surprising that doubts can afflict us on anything short of the penultimate ground of thought. Even the ultimate logical truth is not perfectly satisfying. Only the vision of pure truth itself immediately present and embraced, can completely still the mind, and because we instinctively look for this fullness, we are uneasy with anything less.

St Thomas draws the parallel between a system of truths and a system of goods. Nothing less than the immediate enjoyment of goodness itself, he holds, can quiet the will. Whatever the conviction with which the reason apprehends the idea of infinite goodness and however heroically the will sets itself to serve it, so long as both are rooted in a world of partial realizations and of means to ends, distractions can always be entertained and found beguiling. Psychologically there is an inner indeterminacy of the will in face of anything that is not the complete good; the power of freedom consists in the ability of coming to a resolution and acting on it. Yet if the will acts at all, then the object of its activity must be something invested with goodness, or, in the scholastic phrase, something that participates in goodness.

Similarly there is an inner indeterminacy of the mind to anything less than the sheer and simple truth, a thing completely true, immediately recognized and intimately present. God alone is such a thing, and the beatific vision alone such a confrontation. For anything less and in any other state the mind is not bound to stir. But if we grant that the mind is acting, as we must, since we are considering mental activity not mental inertia, and suppose that the mind is taking up an attitude either for or against a realist philosophy, we may then pause and enquire, what is the content implicit in every judgement. There is no escaping from *is*: the debate is about its reach.

When we are occupied with special truths, whether principles or conclusions, there can be a moment or even a fairly settled period, when we can withhold assent because of the evidence to the contrary. They are not so complete and compelling that the alternative to them is a blank; their opposite is a contrary, it is not a contradictory of being itself. A teacher of mathematics with a sense of history may have a flicker of doubt merely because it is reported that William of Ockham, who obviously was no fool, thought a world would be possible where triangles were not triangular. For that matter even the statements of fools can be disquieting, for who always so certain of himself as not

G

sometimes to wonder whom the cap fits? Many such doubts may be quickly dispelled, but at least they can arise.

But when we are dealing with evidence itself in the most general sense, with intelligibility and *isness*, what is there to suggest positive doubt? Negative doubt is always possible, not by deciding not to think, but by not deciding to think. Let us repeat that we are not dealing with the charter of this or that school of philosophy, nor of the diverse influences that may either attract us or repel us, the beauty or grimness, the comfort or vogue of a system. We are dealing with the object loading the mind if the mind acts at all, the barest minimum manifested during the purest period of intellectualism.

In treating of special truths, it will be a useful method to set off one position with its denial or alternative, and so to discover the truth by way of contrast and suspense. Such a methodic doubt and the limited application of thesis and antithesis is to be found in nearly every article of the *Summa Theologica*, one of the earliest examples being the statement that God does not exist. But how can this method be adopted at the very start of thought? And if so, is it not a case of let's pretend, of a *per impossibile* argument, not of a real discrimination and a solid doubt.

For instance we can suspect the principle of contradiction only in virtue of the principle of contradiction itself, or more precisely, in virtue of its positive counterpart, the principle of identity. Philosophers who profess the doubt of first principles do so, not from a severely formal analysis, but rather from an elevated sentiment of the supreme reality of change and becoming as against a static rest and being, a respect for novelty as against sameness.

Nevertheless the original data of thought should be subjected to a critical appreciation, even if what is primary has to be analysed in terms of what is secondary, and the thing has arrived for good before it is critically reflected on. That is the way the human mind works. Philosophy is scarcely robust if it has to be muffled against doubts. But the reason cannot go on indefinitely, always trying to prove something by something else—the desire is uneducated, observes St Thomas—but must ultimately stop at a truth that is its own evidence. Yet in the meantime, a critical method can be prepared to ditch everything that is intellectually superfluous. For practical reasons we may have to live by certain rules that have not yet been turned inside out, yet to strip thought down to see if there is an indubitable centre is an authentic effort of philosophy.

26. *The* Cogito

In this process of stripping down we have to be careful where we place our doubts, otherwise we shall be as embarrassed as was the post-office assistant when Sir Herbert Tree, after buying a penny stamp, asked, 'And have you no others?' Then attentively scrutinizing the sheet that was produced he pointed to the stamp in the very middle and said, 'I'll take that one.' Something of the sort befell the followers of Descartes who attempted to defend a realist philosophy after doubting that anything existed except the self.

We may accumulate doubts about everything, it was argued, but there still remains the fact that I doubt. I may even doubt my doubting, but I am always involved in the statement that I doubt. *Cogito ergo sum:* I think, therefore I am.

Will this serve as a hard little core of realism, surviving when all else has been swept away; and can it be used as the point of departure from which other truths can be deduced? When men began to think along these lines, they looked for a simple and irreducible affirmation on which to construct an uncontrovertible philosophy—an Escorial of a system, the lonely desert place and on it the geometrical gridiron of rooms.

Danger ahead can already be anticipated if all that I am affirming is a statement about my consciousness and if scepticism has been appeased at the price of a surrender. How am I going to escape from my consciousness? True, I have broken one doubt, but I have let in another. My affirmation is a protest echoing back from the walls of my mental prison? I have started talking to myself and until I am interrupted I shall continue talking to myself.

If, however, an object greater than myself is involved then the statement is not just the beginning of a monologue. Now on reflection it seems that my first principle points to an existent, a thing, a fact, not merely to a meaning, a form, a notion. I start with a perception of myself doing something and end with a reality not limited to my particular reality. The process can be stated thus: *I* think, therefore I *am*. The *cogito* loses much of its force when it is made too exact and qualified, for clearness and definition can be gained at the expense of depth and force. Descartes himself contrasted the crystal clearness of mind with the density of matter. But once we are enclosed in the individuality of the perception we shall never validly be able to enlarge from it to other things. It seems that the stress in the argument should be laid on its generality: that may seem a vaguer start, but it may well prove a stronger. As already noticed in speaking of being in general, there is a modesty about wide and sweeping generalizations that may be lacking in particular asseverations and judgements committed to particular points of fact, though the reverse is commonly taken for granted.

The argument can then be translated as follows: activity, therefore being. The activity happens to be revealed in my consciousness that I am doubting: the being is implied in the same datum.

A similar residue is precipitated in the perceptions we form about what we take to be extra-mental objects. It would seem that the original and simplest form of such statements is to say 'that is green' rather than 'I have the sentiment of a green object'; to say 'I am apprehending something' rather than 'I am apprehending that I am apprehending something.' When we are applying ourselves to particular statements a habit of close and self-critical reflection will of course make us guarded: we shall preface them with 'it strikes me that' and cap them with 'or so it seems to me.'

It is the latter phrase added to what we say that best expresses the situation. The downright statement precedes the qualification: as the scholastics say, *simpliciter* antedates *secundum quid*, an absolute is conceived before a relative is stated. Behind the diffidence of our particular asseverations we can push back to a primitive dogmatism, and what is revealed there is not self-consciousness but the perception of being. Otherwise there can be no positive doubt, which requires the possession of a datum, or rather of data. We shall see in the following chapter that criticism uses particular and positive concepts and applies to the development of our thinking, not to the beginning of knowledge.

In other words, it appears that we start by thinking metaphysically rather than epistemologically, that is to say we think *being* rather than think *about our thinking of being*. Epistemology is not the first but the second part of metaphysics: this is borne out by the history of philosophy, for thought at first was mainly occupied with settling the nature of the external world and it was not until afterwards that the various schools of scepticism arose. In philosophy, as in the unpremeditated humours of conversation between friends, the thought and saying are simultaneous. Direct knowledge precedes reflection, for only after we have responded to an object can we turn back to ourselves. Two terms are originally involved—and we are back again at the hint already thrown out, that in a judgement the logical subject and the psychological subject match and are related to one another and to a logical predicate and an objective meaning through the dynamism of *is*: the logical copula, says St Thomas, responds to the act of existence. It comes from the source whence clear ideas themselves well up.

27. *Direct and Reflex*

The statement that the self exists represents as extreme an objectification as the affirmation of being, and in a sense is more ambitious and requires more evidence. For I do not make any sense at all, even to myself, except by my reactions to an environment; the thinking subject has no meaning until filled with an object; such hints as come from us as apart from object are of want and potentiality, not of content and actuality: even the mystics' sense of their own nothingness is relevant here, and what they feel is supported by a scientific analysis of consciousness. What apparently cannot be done is to go back to the mind before it is charged, and the effects of the attempt resemble those of taking a purge on an empty stomach. In reflection on itself the mind knows itself only because it is manifested in activity, and its activity is manifested only because an object is possessed.

We are speaking of scientific introspection. There is another datum dwelt on by St Augustine, a deeper and less articulate consciousness of the self, an awareness continuously present though not explicitly stated, though even that is recognized only when the mind is acting. No created mind, however noble and however immediate and inborn its insight of reality, is the principle of being as such. Were we free from the peculiar limitations of a mind imbedded in matter we should still not expect to find at the heart of our mental activity the centre and source of evidence, but only a creaturely receptivity, which is perceived when energised by an appropriate existent. We know ourselves in knowing something else other than our own emptiness, and whatever this other may be, it ultimately beckons to God. All conscious things, observes St Thomas, know God implicitly in everything they know.

The deliberate and scientific procedure of introspection, proceeding by delicate and careful enquiry from object to activity, from activity to ability, from ability to subject, is rather a perusal of the nature of the activity and the subject engaged than a judgement as to their existence; it is the psychological attempt to find a meaning rather than to establish a fact; an affair, says St Thomas, of *quid sit*, not an *an sit*, which goes to show that in this context a judgement that something exists belongs rather to direct than to reflexive knowledge.

Of course there is a difference between knowing a truth and knowing that we know the truth, between knowing as knowing and knowing as known. It is in the nature of a supple and spiritual reality to be able to bend back on itself without dislocation and not merely to know but also to know that it knows, and this indeed is the complete self-possession and possession of another of intellectual knowledge. The epistemological issue, which appears when we look critically at knowledge, involves then a reflection on the original activity of knowing, a turning inwards of the mind on its acting self. But this presupposes some previous attention to the nature of being and existence. We must know an object before we can know whether we are knowing. Thus epistemology may present the first problem of philosophy, but not the first question.

On the other hand, if the consciousness of the self is taken as the original and indubitable starting point of theory, it will be found that as nothing is supposed to come in then nothing can come out. We may set out to be realists, but we shall find that we are like the men who thought to increase the food supply by introducing the rabbit to Australia.

28. *Mind in Nature*

One of the causes which made the problem of knowledge such a sharp anxiety has been the separation of knowing from living. The problem seems not to arise in communities living close to the soil and serving the cult of fertility in work and worship and play. We cannot go back to a peasantry, yet it is a commonplace that the advance of civilization brings with it a lack of confidence as gifted individuals separate themselves by their private intellectualism from their solidarity with the mass. The task of a vital philosophy is not to arrest the progress of knowledge, but to keep it rooted in ordinary conditions of reality. There is a kind of sublimity that should be suspected, in thought as in religion; criticism creates gaps that should not be allowed to widen, and that later criticism should close.

The same danger lurks in many places; in the augustinian doctrine that biological claims and spiritual forces move on different planes and in opposing directions; in the platonic conflict between errant and necessary causes; in the opposition between nature and morals and nature and law, with the consequent elaboration of law without any reference to nature or morals; in the false contrasts between religion and politics when the following concepts are not properly matched, eternal, bodily, ecclesiastical, secular, spiritual, temporal, civil, sacred.

In approaching the criticism of knowlege what should be shunned from the outset is setting thoughts apart from things, and erecting the former into objects of contemplation and then expecting them to throw light on a dark and fundamentally unmental world of matter. Separate thought from things and you have set a conundrum that otherwise would not crop up. It is like splitting the soul from the body, or rather the body from the soul, and then having to face the consequences of a divided life. Better to confuse name and object, as primitive realism is accused of doing. This dualism has struck deep into the theory of knowledge; its immediate historical background was the cartesian separation of spirit and matter, each running on lines that according to some appear to touch in an unexplained manner, or, according to others, on lines that run parallel. Instead both should be seen as different manifestation of an analogically identical reality.

Now before seeking to close the gap, we may remark that such dualism is alien to the temper of the aristotelean and thomist philosophy: distinctions are made there in abundance, but they are not driven so hard as to become an opposition of irreconcilable entities. The mentalist problem does not arise partly because the psychological climate is not favourable. In some places St Thomas takes knowledge as the highest development of life and in other places, as in the *Summa Theologica*, the nature of life is the topic immediately following the enquiry into the nature of truth—the way, the truth, the life, all are one.

The situation for a mentalist is different. He assumes that the first objects of the mind are ideal or mental conditions, and he fears that these may be quite different from the outside stuff of reality. He may set out to bridge the chasm because his intentions are realist, with a theory of correspondence if he be a cartesian, with the postulates of the practical reason if he be a kantian, but there is always a chasm: a calculus is set on one side, an irreducible welter on the other; light on one side, murk on the other.

The attempt to set ideas in relation to things is bound to have doubtful success so long as both are regarded as belonging to fundamentally antagonistic and self-contained worlds, not as shuttling in and out of one another, interlacing and interpenetrative, different variations of the same reality. Unless attended by the high conviction that pure being at the top consists in pure knowing—the *esse per se subsistens* of some thomists is the *verum per se intelligens* of others—and at the bottom in a respect for the artless sincerity of straight sensations we are laying ourselves open to the doubts of mentalism. Even when our concepts are confident and practicable, so long as they are taken as things in their own right they are rather like the members of Jewish or Catholic communities in a modern nation-state—loyal enough, but not utterly committed, and therefore not completely reliable.

Indirect realism is the historical predecessor of that idealism which in its turn precedes solipsism, or the doctrine that the self is quite alone. The connection, which is corroborated by the succession of events in the history of philosophy, is partly contained in the logic of ideas. If the first object of our knowledge is a thought then presently this thought will become the exclusive object of our knowledge. Thought will be our think-thing, and how then are we to get to thing-thing, and how can we even think thing-thing?

The impasse was presented to the western mind on a grand scale in the early middle ages by the famous demonstration of St Anselm for the existence of God, an argument that was to be restated by Descartes and Leibniz centuries later. It is an argument that may be too readily dismissed as a play on words, for it brings to a head the whole problem of knowledge, and certainly for a man who is convinced that our thoughts are the only things we can be certain about there must be periods when he finds the argument almost impossible to refute. St Anselm addressed the argument to men who already believed in the existence of God, and in fairness to him it should be said that the argument can have retrospective validity. Since his time it has been addressed to an audience that has embarked on transcendental speculation, and therefore should find it at least worrying. A hearty positivist is left completely cold.

The argument may be stated as follows. The very concept of God implies the idea of existence, for by universal agreement it signifies that than which nothing greater can be thought of, and thus by definition must be thought of as actually existing, for otherwise we could think of a greater.

It has been said that St Thomas performs a similar transformation act of mental into real when in his fourth proof for the existence of God he argues to the existence of an absolute perfection from the different degrees of perfection we can range in our mind. Yet the criticism is unfounded, for he does not argue from purely mental comparatives to an extra-mental superlative. This danger was surely in his mind, for only just before giving his own argument he had criticized the anselmic argument for making an illegitimate jump from the ideal to the real.

The argument as it existed in St Anselm's mind is another matter, for he was talking in a theocentric culture, habituated to the verbal usages, mental habits, conventions, and motions of a believing community, and despite his slight concern with the empirical he was not offering his argument *in vacuo*, as a piece of eliminatory abstraction according to logical analysis. Allowing for this we should note the profound difference between the two arguments, despite their syntactic similarity. For whereas the anselmic argument does start from a notion, the *quarta via* of St Thomas begins from an induction establishing the existence of limited and graded things, and then proceeds to deduce the existence of an unlimited and supreme being. The fallacious transition of the anselmic argument is also performed by philosophies that would infer the existence of a real world from the analysis of mental forms. But while the process of St Thomas may or may not be more cogent, it is certainly different, for it at least claims to start from the perception of existing things; and this applies to all philosophies that recognize that the human mind can never breed an existent unless previously fertilized from existence.

The physical world may have been worldliness to the early medieval philosophers, yet by the thirteenth century it was a real interest and a proper object for the play of philosophical wisdom. Though many still agreed with St Augustine that the sincerity of truth was not to be looked for in the senses and some succumbed to the philosophical temptation of withdrawing to ideas from the insecurity of sensation, others showed themselves solicitous for the philosophical status of facts and set themselves to base the highest speculation on full empirical activity. Among them were St Thomas and Scotus, the latter indeed on this point departed from the venerable tradition of his order and criticised the theory that knowledge comes by illumination from above.

Scholasticism cannot justly be represented as the elaboration of mental counters, for running through the movement was a strong sense of fact; in metaphysics there was sturdy insistence on the data of sensation, in the ethics on the physical nature of human drives. Neither science was a tidy exploration of neat premisses; there was a precious absence of uplift and rhetorical façade, and not without point is the medieval fable that Gratian the father of canon law and Peter Lombard the father of scholastic theology were brothers, and both born out of wedlock.

Yet the ideal of a united experience and philosophical theory did not last, the fourteenth century went off into a logic of words, and by the time of Malebranche the *sacra doctrina* had retreated back again into the cloister and the life of the spirit had withdrawn from the world and left the explanation of physical reality to the mechanists. Religion became a sentiment and metaphysics

a mood, science a technique and literature a trade; the harmony
was broken and all that was left were snatches of song and bits of
the score: that is an overstatement, but not by much.

As christian morals may survive after christian doctrines have
been rejected so realism may remain long after its speculative
capital has been spent. Yet indirect realism can scarcely avoid
subjectivism if we press the logic of its ideas to their utmost,
which, as Newman noted, men seldom do. A single argument,
like a single human act, such as a murder, may take a lifetime.

The classical formula from the eighteenth century is *esse est
percipi*, being is being perceived. Berkeley himself was not a
realist in either the Ionian or the materialist sense of the word,
yet he would have disavowed the later philosophies that derived
from his philosophy, the doctrine of the individual lost in a
solitary dream or seeking to sink himself in unconsciousness. He
was re-stating the old religious platonism of the divine ideas.
'All the choir of heaven and furniture of earth—in a word all
those bodies which compose the mighty frame of the world—
have not any subsistence without a mind.' St Augustine had
argued along the same lines, and though rejecting the opinion that
what is true is what appears because stones hidden in the bowels
of the earth would not be true stones because they are unseen,
his analysis of reality takes him back to the exemplars existing in
the mind of God.

But if this was all very well for the great visionaries, the more
humdrum course lay in saying that being is being perceived and
this meant being perceived by our minds since we know no other.
Logical analysis should stop at that, leaving it open whether or
not there was a transcendental consciousness or an absolute unconsciousness or just blankly nothing.

Without accepting the radical cleavage between thoughts and
things, a criticism of such mentalism may however be conducted
on its own presuppositions, and by applying a critical doubt, its
contention may be convicted of logical short-comings. For example in the argument:

no idea can exist apart from mind;
but, every known thing is an idea;
therefore, no known thing can exist apart from mind:—

there is an equivocation in the middle term that may slip past too easily. In the major premiss *idea* stands for a thought-thing, while in the minor premiss idea stands for a thing-thought. The first statement means that as a mental state an idea is in the mind, which is, of course, a truism: the second statement says that what we know is an idea, and this is precisely in debate—we may remind ourselves that begging the question is a fallacy only when inserted into an argument. The shade of difference between the two senses of the term, though slight in appearance, is sufficient to invalidate the argument.

The passage from the *percipi* to the *esse* presents no puzzle, for at the beginning why should a separation between them be presumed? There is no primitive evidence for it in fact, and in theory it is unthinkable. Is it not precisely the absence of radical division between thought as such and reality as such, the impossibility of holding them apart in order to equate them, that allows us to feel that there is a catch somewhere? Light and heat are conjoined in fire, the eye does not doubt the one nor the touch the other, but they are not so close as being and being true, thing and thing known, which are originally, and before human consciousness, identical and convertible terms. At a later stage of knowledge, one set of data, which are called thoughts, may be separated from another set, which are gestured at and called things. When thinking grows more fine-spun it is inevitable that things should then appear veiled or resistant, and as judgements branch out and are systematized and specialism develops this or that aspect, the opposition, and even the disparity, between thoughts and things becomes more pronounced. The more thoughts take on an exclusively logical character the more they are set off against the fuller and untidier conditions of reality.

But a distinction is not an exclusion, though the human mind labours under the constant temptation of plumping for one or other of the extremes when striking a contrast. Before thought grows reflexive and pointedly logical, and while the mind is still taking things in its stride, there are no grounds for supposing that it is utterly different from its object. A true thing, says St Thomas, and a thing are not different except logically; and he tilts at the notion that truth is a special kind of being, or that it adds anything extraneous to being. It is a general mode conse-

quent on all being given a mind that contains being. The
existential reference in primitive knowledge is not an extraneous
denomination or an outside reference somehow tagged on to it,
as when we say *east of Bombay* or *State-insured*, but enters into the
heart of the matter, as when we say the *breath of life* or the *glow of
health.*

Later on rifts may appear between our thoughts and what we
suppose to be things; and then, and not before, the methods of indirect realism are useful for testing the correspondence between
our perceptions and the objects we perceive. They may have the
effect of disturbing our complacency in many cases when it is
shown that things are not what they appear. Granting for purposes of argument that appearances are frequently deceptive, the
fundamental doctrine of realism still lies much farther back,
behind such specialized questions as the veracity of our senses, or
whether the scene in front of us is just what a countryman would
take it to be, elms and sheep and so forth, or whether it is a collection of bunches of sub-atomic energy swarming like midges, or
merely the mathematical patterns of some mind in an inexplicable
fashion spilling over into sensuousness.

The contrast struck between scepticism and mentalism is
rough and ready, but convenient. The sceptic suffers from an
inability to affirm, even, in extreme cases, his own thoughts,
though in practice he breaks out through his affections, his herd
consciousness, the compulsion to adjust himself in most matters
to what is generally agreed on. The mentalist may abound with
affirmations, but when pressed can produce no convincing speculative reasons for the existence of a world outside his mind. He
is also influenced by many factors that make him discharge his
debts as well as other men, and both he and the sceptic can admit
that life can be lived on a basis of probability, though probability
is resolved into factors without much intellectual force. We may
be like the church at Sardis, which passes for a living man yet all
the while is a corpse, and so, unless we have a realist philosophy,
we may think that we are engaged in a dialectic when all the time
we are talking to ourselves.

It might have proved suicidal of living thought were the mind
not so meekly tough that almost any liberties can be taken with
it—it is like human nature with regard to sin and beautiful even

in dilapidation. We can see now that mentalism has served a most useful purpose. When it was most dominant an observer might have been excused for fearing that never again would philosophy recapture the realist spirit of an earlier age—we speak of metaphysical realism, not of the realism of positivism, which lies in an avoidance of metaphysics, and proceeds on its way unperturbed by transcendental doubts. It was as if metaphysics had lost its virginity and would never be the same again. But knowledge and love do not obey the laws of the flesh, and as in morals penitence may recover the heart of virtue despite past material incidents, and may even be happier in the event. Gregory says of Mary Magdalene, that she sought for him she had not found and saw him when the others were away.

The philosophical tradition may be little the worse for its adventure, and even after recovery all the better for its lapse. Digestion is the better for ferments and philosophy is the better for friction, and now for the future realism can have a rasp in its thought and the resolve of never again. Yet the process of recovery may be painful, as, in some ways, a man recovering his sanity suffers more than when he was going mad, and people say that artificial respiration is an agony compared with drowning.

29. *Stages of Realism*

Critical and indirect realism developed partly because it was felt that naive and direct realism was an unreasoned acceptance of the way most of us think and act, a matter-of-factness which may or may not be rationalized on pragmatic grounds. On the other hand we have seen the dangers that lay in too uncritical an acceptance of the existence of the problem, or rather in misplacing the doubt. As communities need rebels, or at least free venturers, if they are not to stagnate, so the tradition of philosophy may advance because doubt and darkness have supervened to assurance and day. After the subjectivism that followed from the too Gallic objectivism of the seventeenth century we may look to see if there is a third stage of realism, a realism that is direct but not naive, critical but not indirect, a philosophy that may have lost the childlikeness of the medievals but has recovered their confidence.

It will be direct inasmuch as it does not start by saying that there are two parallel streams, of thoughts and of things, and then attempting either to make them meet or to run alongside one another, like the Bedford Level by the channel of the Ouse. It discerns that being lies in the very beginning of knowledge and that the first act of the mind is a statement of something other than itself; it recognizes that we cannot unthink ourselves out of this affirmation of being.

It will also be critical inasmuch as it is prepared to work back by reflections to the first elements of knowledge and there expose a transcendental object. We are in the middle of the drama and not at the beginning, and only by an effort of mind can we prevent the relapse into chaos and black night; this philosophical realism will not be unprepared to engage opponents with the weapons of mentalist logic.

It is implicit in the philosophy of Aristotle and St Thomas. Scepticism they knew, but they wrote before there was anything like the great anxiety that descended on western philosophy for two or three centuries. Consequently their realism, though philosophical, is performed rather than solemnized, or, as the scholastics would say, is expressed *in actu exercito* rather than *in actu signato*. For the same reason in Plato a criticism of knowledge is disentangled with difficulty from his general metaphysics. We may say that in a sense the ancient and medieval realist philosophers had never lost their metaphysical innocence.

But there are shades of realism as there are shades of black. A realist may be like Francis Webb, the famous engineer of Crewe: the directors, he growled, may have any colour they like for the company's engines, so long as it is black. And the result was the beautiful blackberry sheen of the old London and North Western. So a critical realist may be direct, but with a difference. The following chapters will be an attempt to build up the position in layers.

We are out to possess a metaphysical realism which is not quite the same as the ordinary scientific realism of cleaned-up commonsense or the realism which serves as the charter for positivism. It will be gratifying if philosophical realism is in the event able to provide a background for the sciences, though if we set out with this main intention our procedure will be rather like roasting a joint in order to eat it cold.

Yet we should adopt the mood of schooling ourselves to the laws that reality may exhibit. We are part of a bigger world, we should not be the centre of our environment even to ourselves. Our natural desires are responses to objects that are already there. If we set ourselves to like what we get we may find that we shall get what we like. Anyhow we shall not make a solitude and call it peace.

CHAPTER VI

THE BUILD UP

IN stages that may recall the passage from the Ionians past the Sophists to Socrates and thence to Plato and Aristotle—from object through subject to concept and thence to idea and embodied nature—the doctrine of direct yet critical realism may be set out. Five periods can be marked and five demands. First, that there is an impulse within us to make absolute affirmations; second, that it springs from inside the mind and is not mainly contributed by the will; third, that the act of the mind is itself a reply to a challenge; fourth, that the object is set over and against the human mind. The following chapter will touch on the fifth period, of criticism.

When discussing our response to what may be known and loved it will make for tidiness to distinguish between the *other*, the *objective*, the *external*, and the *extrinsic*, of which the first three, and to some extent the fourth, may well eventually coincide though at first separately considered. This division, far from being an unnecessary refinement, is rather a crude simplification, for the parts are interpenetrating and throw out many other branches.

We may say briefly that the *other* confronts the self in a thou-me relationship possibly above and certainly apart from the critical problem as stated by philosophers: here is the mystic's situation, and though he may not frame it in words, if he does, he will variously describe the self, as emptiness, or as a true reality in though not of itself, or as a co-operating agent, depending on his incidental philosophy, neo-platonic, thomist, or molinist as the case may be, or perhaps depending on the stress demanded by the occasion of his experience. He is not concerned to set forth an epistemological doctrine, for he is in a mystery, not a problem.

The *objective* is paired with the *subjective* and, though both terms are analogical and exhibit different shades and intensities of meaning according to their setting in logic or critical philosophy, we may say that in general they are part of the premises of a rational enquiry. *External* contrasts with *internal*, and with these terms we descend to the lower reaches of philosophy as it enters the region of material nature; they belong to the psychology of knowledge. *Extrinsic* again is a more restricted term; contrasting with *intrinsic* it belongs to what may be called the biology of knowledge and is engaged when we discuss whether knowledge is a layer deposited from without or to what extent it is a vital projection.

In other words, the mystic absorbed in the *other* might be at a loss for an answer, or feel that the question is irrelevant, when asked whether the other is objective. Again, a non-subjectivist philosopher might hesitate to declare that the object of his knowledge is external, he might even hesitate as to whether it was real as opposed to mental. Similarly a non-idealist philosopher is not forced to conclude that knowledge is drawn from the mechanical and chemical changes caused by extrinsic physical objects in sense-organs. The writer is persuaded that the other is objective, that the objective is external, and that the external is in part presented through the basic sense of touch, but there are at least four separate considerations here, and in discussing the reality of knowledge it is important to indicate the system of reference.

30. *Impulse to Certitude*

A hankering for danger and discovery is not uncommon among Europeans, but even an explorer has something to go on. He is not flotsam drifting from nowhere. Excitement is set against a background of rules. Taking risks recognizes the force of certain factors. A dinghy can be sailed with dash, but it is foolish to rock the boat. Even a gambler who throws for the highest stakes is prepared to abide by the etiquette. And so a man can philosophize with verve without making a cult of insecurity or seeking to question everything indefinitely.

Glamour flickers over the adventure of scepticism, especially with a fire in the panelled room: patronage is easy from the comfort of regular meals and the run of a library. Romance is one thing, reading romances another; vagabondage is one thing, fireside travels another. Some of the philosophies of protest seem about as charged with suffering as is a genteel pastel of St Francis feeding the birds, in a room curtained with chintz and strewn with pouffes. An irresponsible philosophism toying elegantly with doubts about urgent needs and dear and harsh convictions can be like an armchair revolutionary blandly shrugging over the thuggery that will be let loose. Unfortunately the critics survive the tragic intellectuals, like the defeatists who come out into public life again when the men who fought are buried in the desert or the sea.

Anybody who writes about the problem, rather than in the problem, must feel shamefaced for his flow of words when in his vitals he should be sharing his brother's agony. Scepticism can still be played as a parlour game, as once it was a smart Athenian pastime, and publicists can still make some reputation from it, like the sophists scorned by Plato—'shopkeepers with spiritual wares.' Nor are sceptics alone condemned, but also the chubby and easy optimists, who thrive in the shadow of righteousness; these are like the money changers in the temple. A cheerful and ironical scepticism serves a purpose when it salts the heavy insipidities of earnest metaphysicians. There are drolleries in the highest subjects, as the scholastics well knew. The really haggard sceptics are the victims of metaphysics, as men in despair are the victims of religion. Yet while they dumbly face their doom or rage seeking what they may find they bear witness to their hunger for perfection, not to nothingness, a restlessness that will not be satisfied with what is superficial and secondary, but only with what is profound and primary.

Scepticism may sparkle from a certain dryness of temperament, the fiery element of Heraclitus that will not tolerate the waxen cold of death, and from a liveliness impatient with the inertia of conventional dogma, but that it is fundamentally intellectual may well be doubted. Unable to suffer fools gladly what is there left to suffer? Or it may come from a desire to be invulnerable and immune, and hence avoids pledging itself to anything. Or it may be a movement for the abolition of desire. But annihilation is no end; we cannot strain at nought; the will for extinction is at worst the refusal of something and at best the denial of the petty because we have not found the perfect.

There is evidence here of a desire without reserve. Such

scepticism is really a tension waiting for the affirmation and possession of the absolute, the state of refusing to be fobbed off with relative affirmations. Even if the doubt is not affirmed the need of affirmation may still be evident. Happiness is the sign of what is right, even bogus enjoyment holds something at its core, and a fundamental sceptic may at least try to learn a dignified apathy in his unhappiness.

A natural desire is prophetic in its activity, and even in lethargy is a speaking pain. A pointless drive makes no desire and its absence is no grief. Nature does nothing in vain, said the scholastics; and Sir Thomas Browne, 'there are no Grotesques in Nature'; and John Locke, 'nature never makes excellent things for mean or no uses.' When they spoke of a natural desire they meant it in no animist sense, as in the poetry of 'spears yearning to damage flesh.' They meant that reaching out is inexplicable unless there be an end; they were not speaking from an empty optimism, but from a conviction of teleology and a severe analysis of its implications.

These rational measures apply to everything in our world and they offer some of the best clues as to what this world is about. Not least when the subject is the human mind, where, underneath the curiosity and irreverence and admiration, and even in the streak of wildness, there is a profound drive to certainty, not so much for comfort as for the sake of its own integrity in the possession of an unqualified object.

31. Burden of Mind

Though supported by other interests and desires, the thrust for assurance is intellectual. To some the mind left to itself appears too quizzical and reserved a power to set things moving; they point to the classical difference between cognition and appetition: whereas the former is satisfied with the presence of an object according to a mental mode of being, the latter presses outward to secure the naked presence of its object. Hence after the pure reason has drawn up its theoretical schemes and done with its criticisms, which are but the arrangements of concepts after all, then another impulse breaks in, driving us to mingle in the real life of things. This impulse may be rationalized afterwards, in terms either of success or of a value that merits our entire service.

Pragmatism we have already noticed; disbelieving the ability of the theoretical mind to reach things as they are, it substitutes for the speculative certainty of a plan possessed in advance the practical working certainty of feeling that you are rather enjoying what you are doing or have found that you have been justified by success. It carries the spirit of utilitarianism, free and easy rather than contrived and calculating.

Lying to the other extreme, though characterized by a similar disbelief in pure intellectualism, is another doctrine that would open the way to an unreserved affirmation, namely, the categoric moral imperative of right, of duty for duty's sake. Here is a truth supposedly not demonstrable yet undeniable, lifted above self-seeking desire and self-regarding criticism, an absolute to be sought with disinterested energy. And from this high value of a moral law revealed in our conscience much can be deduced; the freedom of the will, for otherwise duty does not make sense; the existence of God the legislator and the immortality of the soul, for we do not make the law of altruism, and only in an afterlife can the claims of duty be fulfilled. No scientific conclusion of the materialist method, it is argued, can tell against these deeply personal convictions.

Such was one way of surpassing theoretic doubts. There were others, some lyrical, some more dionysical. But all have this in common, that the assent to an unqualified object is fundamentally not an act of the mind at all but an act of love, possibly an act of will, perhaps an act of choice. Our thoughts arise from what we are doing, what we are doing is decided by what we want, and they are prospectively justified by what we are going to do. Believe and you may make it so. Taste and see. Modern propaganda makes a caricature of these partially valid principles and is launched from the fact that if you say a thing strongly and frequently enough you will make others believe it and possibly come to believe it yourself. But the principles of an affective philosophy have a better warrant in our feeling that trust and confidence are a result rather of character than of intelligence.

Successful communities are the confident ones, the groups not given over to doubts, possessing a common faith, even if that be only in the worth of settled property or in the expectation of the indefinite expansion of markets, as in Georgian England and Teddy

Roosevelt America. Some forms of religion appear to show that a system may be speculatively baseless and superstitious, and yet irreproachable from the point of view of the medical psychologist. Faith would not be shaken were it proved that christianity compared very unfavourably with primitive polynesian religion in this respect. Hitler tried to produce a group confidence similar to that of the English, which he admired, but his subjects seemed to lack psychological carelessness and ability to play; their claim to innocence was the result of an unadjusted disturbance and was expressed in arrogance, very different from the understated assurance of Queen Victoria's private who was threatened with protracted death unless he kow-towed to his captors: 'We don't do that in the Buffs,' he said simply, and so was turned over to the torturers.

A healthy community moves as a whole. Its members will themselves be healthy when they are acting in unison. In such a state our real personality is expressed in our social life and not in our privacy, and we should not withdraw into a private commentary of doubts, perhaps protesting that everybody is out of step except ourselves. And so, it is urged, anybody with good dispositions and a sense of what is owing to the community will be a realist. Philosophy becomes a moral matter, and its conclusions will be praised in the name of goodness rather than of truth.

By concentrating on the part played by appetite we cannot blink the fact that any meaning present in the situation comes from the intelligence. Looked at merely as a movement, a transference of energy, love is like the tide or a bird-eating plant or any other forms of aggrandisement. What kind of appetite I have, its form, meaning, and human interest, is decided by the knowledge within it. Though a decision of will may be required to break the stalemate of doubt, appetitive factors by themselves furnish no evidence. They may be the push, but they are not the entrance. They have to be suffused with meaning to have any human relevance, though that meaning need not be of the type that can be set out in didactically rational terms. Our desires may prompt the need of affirmation, but they are not affirmations themselves. The wish is not the father to the thought, the thought is the father to the wish. Appetite alone makes motion, not sense; such causality as it possesses is efficient, not formal.

By drawing this distinction between intellectualism and

voluntarism, the current opposition between a rather bleak and arid finding of explanations and a warmer adhesion to reality is not necessarily endorsed, nor the contrast between scholastic theory of the highest and driest condition and affective theology, between the academic institutes and the schools of the devout life. For within the mind itself there is an inner natural gravitation, an intellectual *pondus naturae*, bearing nearer to existents than any choice; and in every motion the will must observe the distance from its object prescribed by the reason.

There is an inner impotence within the power of affection, an inability to secure and grasp by itself what is loved. If there be possession, this can come only through an act of knowledge. The begotten is not love, St Augustine says, but the principle of love; the scholastic theologians discovered when they came to the Trinity that the *processio amoris* carries no special name. It may well be that the mind is accused of coldness, not because of its own inner desire, which is currently neglected in the discussion of the topic, but because of the separateness of the will from its object in its earliest motions. The mind is alive before moving into the realm of deliberations and choices; it has started to look for intelligibility long before reasons are articulated in scientific phrases; at the spring of philosophy there is an impulse within the mind, and we shall misread its nature if we think that it is an affair of the head alone: the mind, says St Thomas, is entire in every part of the body, and it philosophizes best when the heart is knowing and the head is loving.

A strict intellectualism, then, is not enamoured of braininess nor need it treat the intelligence as a self-sufficient power able to guarantee itself apart from the organism. Possibly endemic malaria did as much as anything to sap the high speculation of the Greeks, and we have already noted that the most aspiring metaphysics is based on the humblest needs, and that not merely because there are plain necessities previous to rationalism: as the scholastics said, *prius vivere quam philosophari*, food comes first. So then there is no question, certainly for an aristotelean, of holding that the problem can be solved by the exercise of pure reason. Yet he does require that at the decisive point the solution should turn on an activity of the mind. The mind is made for seeing, not for obeying; to adopt evidence not to submit to pressure.

What should be avoided is to make philosophy repose on a belief. Faith is inherently blind: it issues from the confrontation of the mind with a truth that does not communicate its own evidence. The object may be highly credible and vouched for by strong intellectual guarantees, but these good and sufficient reasons lie outside the inner object of the assent; and this assent, when it comes to the point, is determined by a choice. The reasons are also good in the sense that they promote the good life, for faith, certainly in its higher reaches, is essentially a virtue of morality—not indeed that it is modulated by reasonable living, but that it charges the power of right action and ensures its exercise. Merely as an intellectual quality it comes, as St Thomas notes, lowest in the scale of unwavering assents, and as such cannot be called a virtue at all.

It is not surprising of course that moral philosophers have demanded that goodwill should initiate philosophy. We should accept the responsibility of having a mind, and as the very name suggests, philosophy demands that we should be lovers of wisdom rather than certificated sages. Historically the development of a philosophy starts in the life of the individual with a special act of the will and as a tradition from the personal influence of a few commanding characters on the life of the community; it does not seem that philosophy can be formed by a group-pressure, though this is necessary to allow the conditions of free speculation. As such it is bound up with the play of free-will, accepting the responsibility for how we act and the obligation for giving a reason for what we do. Nevertheless the content of our first affirmation cannot be evidentially resolved into such choices.

Nor should we expect the first principles of philosophy to be held by an effort of will. Even the religious life cannot be carried on by will-power alone for any length of time without a breakdown, and religion is the service of a mystery, whereas philosophy, though more unassuming, requires for its tranquillity a visual assent of the mind to the inner evidence of its principles. That what is seen is less than the highest is part of its strength: pure intelligences enjoying the vision of truth have no need of metaphysics, which is a human need.

Appetites will reinforce the assent, and all human abilities should work together in building up the system. Ideas will spill into action, and action will disclose further ideas. The theory and doctrine will prove to work out in practice—in the long run—and to be supported by the convergence of a multitude of probabilities. All intellectual truth leads to or holds the lasting and authentic good, the ultimate *bonum honestum*, the thing of worth, the object decent to the mind, and this also is the *bonum delectabile*, the thing of delight, the satisfaction to desire. But truth comes first, and goodness next, while beauty, as Eric Gill said, will take care of herself.

32. *The Reply to Another*

Having reached the point that philosophy starts with an affirmation of mind rather than of will, the next step is to investigate whether this assent is evoked by an object other than the human mind, an object to that extent non-mental. For one might well agree that the first assent is intellectual yet at the same time look upon its target as a projection of the reason or of some wider or world-consciousness in which human minds are somehow caught up. The persuasion that mental objects are of our own fabrication carries on and fills out the old saying of Protagoras that man is the measure of all things. It is argued that however far back we probe, all that is stated in consciousness cannot be shown to be anything else than the product of the mind's own activity.

The dialectic of rationalist subjectivism has different nuances. The conclusion may be regretted and the sentiment of Quarles approved:

> No man is born unto himself alone;
> Who lives unto himself, he lives to none.

Or again, the existence of an outside world and something of its nature may be shrewdly suspected on non-rationalist grounds. Or again, the assertion that everything we think we know is an extrapolation of the human mind itself may be vigorously maintained without apology.

Then why should the mind affirm? One answer might be that we cannot help ourselves. There is no reason for it; the mind happens to be like that and cannot help following its own blind and involuntary compulsions. Does the object we call a tree in

our minds ask itself why it grows up to what we call the light?
This, of course, is no sort of explanation, nor is it seriously meant
for one; it is an example of that taciturn determinism which says
that things happen just because they happen to happen, and why
ask? But we do ask, the question of certitude is not to be shrugged
off.

Another answer, scarcely more helpful, postulates an obscure
and profound consciousness which is the principle of our affirmations. Clear and rational consciousness does but embroider on
that mysterious sympathy. That this is a fair enough description
of what happens may well be the case, and it is worth recognizing
the rootings of our conscious mind deep into the unconscious.
The rational mind is healthy only on condition that it continues,
or at least respects, the biological drives that start from there. It
flourishes when it is affirming. But we ask, though we may be
disappointed, is it not possible to have explanatory evidence at
this point, not just an exclamation at a mysterious profundity?

There are, of course, brisker and more serviceable reasons. The
dogmatic tendency is the result of the pressure of custom. We
know little about congenital drives, but more about educated
habits; little about psychic heredity, more about psychological
environment. Affirmation may not be native to us, but it is
forced on us, encrusted on us as a sort of protective covering.
Inside we are as vagrant and chancy as the breeze, as spumey and
instable as water, but we find that we have to fix ourselves and
be definite in order to fit in with the community. So we congeal
into a covering of convictions and prejudices.

Local and limited as this interpretation may be, it does suppose
an outside world. There is this to be said for such readings and
also for the materialism of conditioned reflexes and the like, that
a sufficiently blunt and imagined realism is taken for granted,
though perhaps it is not sufficiently analysed. In fact a century
ago to be a realist usually meant that you were a positivist as
well. Yet although it is a profitable course to treat perception as
a nervous event to be subjected to objective tests, the positivist
reduction of consciousness to the nervous system, though avoiding
the problems of transcendental philosophy, is death to scientific
philosophy, shrouding the absence of ultimate reasons in a web
of measurement. Let us remind ourselves that the interest of the

metaphysician is to remain scientific and yet go into a world beyond physics.

But to revert to the subjectivist philosophy. Human knowledge is framed in a necessity and cannot function outside that setting. Yet what we take for the outside world does not exhibit any such necessity. A thousand experiences, all similar, do not amount to the statement of a law, unconditioned and exact. We may register approximate repetitions, but the shape and connections of what we experience are furnished by the mind. Moreover it is only by the memory that we know them as repetitions and say that the same self saw one dog yesterday and another to-day. A crude example might be taken from a machine on a railway-station platform into which a ribbon of strip zinc is fed on which we stamp a series of letters making a name: so something from outside may be fed into us, though nothing so known and definite as strip zinc, and on it the reason gives the stamp of meaning.

While this meaning might be taken for a period to constitute the entire occupation of rational philosophy, we notice all the same that something appears to be given from outside. I observe myself closely, and the introspection does not reveal that my primitive consciousness is its own proper object; rather it appears as a means through which something other than itself is known, be this the mental condition of another mind, or of my own mind in another series, or a physical thing. Even when I reflect on my thought, my thinking thought of is not precisely the same as my thinking unthought of.

Then, I also remind myself, other minds besides my own find the same necessity and universality; they deal also with objects that rouse the same doubts; they do not appear to be echoes of me. The mind would not be roused to debate were it the only one in the world: most civilized adults rejoice in the clash of minds, but all are not Mitteleuropans, unhappy when they are not agreed with. The existence of one other mind is sufficient answering object, though of course it is not enough to establish realism in the empirical and positivist sense of the word.

Also we may remark that the more certain our judgements are, even on purely analytic grounds, the more impersonal they seem to be. Moreover they are then not dictated by individual and idiosyncratic desires. Comfort they do not provide, but a purer

sort of rest, a more disinterested peace, the release of great
literature. There it is, a form I have not made. How good it is.
I have found it and admire.

> Cruel, but composed and bland,
> Dumb, inscrutable and grand.

The peace of such objective forms lies in the fact that they are
given, not invented. Their evidence lies in them, not in me. The
inevitability is there, not here.

Who has not felt at moments an object hard and uncaring,
callous but admirable, alien, even hostile, and quite other from
you? When the landscape is not bathed in the hopes of the sight
of your friend, when you have no reassurance in your clothes or
the railway train or in belonging to the contemporary scene, or in
recalling the historic interest and memories in the landscape:
when a cherished scheme has failed, then the mind may see with
a peculiar clarity its own triviality before the granite cliffs
and the perpetual uncaring sea. There is a bitterness at the heart
of philosophy; a sadness, noted by St Thomas, in the middle of
science. All should know it, not the professional philosophers
only, but all who would think rationally and sensitively about
their environment. Warmth departs, pleasure too and even pain;
the mind is stripped of its own inventions and left naked in a
world, not of its own making, but to which it must adjust itself.

33. *The Real Antagonist*

We ask for bread, and shall we be given a stone? A natural
desire is evidence for an object. An ability cannot reach out into
a vacuum. There is no potential without the actual somewhere.
No guarantee is promised that our appetites will in fact be fulfilled, that depends on many factors, but only that the first conditions of fulfilment are present.

In order to introduce extra-mental reality to mind, which is
the fourth stage of our argument, this strain should first be felt, as
of the mind pitted against reality, like Jacob with the angel, who
touched his thigh and left him lame before he blessed him. The
wrestling of mind with nature is like a marriage, and without it
the mind gets into bachelor ways. The religious truth that men
must be wounded before they can enter into the kingdom is a

parable for the gropings of epistemology. The second-born have
no urge to procreate an image of themselves; humanity is not
an idol fit for human worship. But to return to less symbolic
considerations, and more pedestrian ways.

Some judgements merely seem to affirm a relationship of
notions, or rather, they need imply no more; thus that $2+2=4$,
or that whole is greater than part. Others however are statements
of what exists, or make the claim: thus that Adam and Eve were
two people, and Cain and Abel two more, and that the four of
them made a family, and that Cain was less than the group.
Which comes first to the mind, the judgements of abstract and
ideal terms, or the statements of fact? It would seem that once
our minds are trained into the scientific arrangement and development of ideas they are jerked with difficulty back again into the
condition when there was an almost dumb consciousness of an
existent without formal statement.

Later we shall have to examine whether judgements that seem
to be about purely mental relationships do not also contain a
reference to an existent being, but for the present we remain with
a companion who has gone so far with us as to agree that the mind
seeks certainty and indeed may find it in an object other than the
human mind, but hesitates to say that this is anything other than
a form of consciousness or mental entity in another mind, greater
than ours.

He would argue that the first objects of our mind are ideas,
but not our ideas. To a thorough paced idealist, who has surpassed
the mechanical preoccupations of indirect realism, the possibility
of establishing a connection between our mind and a reality independent of mind does not arise: to him it is an unreal question.
For everything relevant to mind is a thought, nothing can be
included in consciousness except objects of consciousness. How
can we seek to compare thoughts with things in the medium of
mind when the latter are unknown quantities and utterly unrelated to mind? How can they be anything else but thoughts?
And if not in our mind then in some other. This mind, according
to an idealist who is also a theist, will be the mind of the first
thinker.

At first a realist feels no call to controvert such a conclusion for
it agrees that there is an object over and against the human mind.

Not until later, and probably not until the discussion has moved into metaphysics proper and then re-entered natural philosophy, does the question arise whether there be things that are not made of mental stuff. Then the all-comprehensive mind of God will not be discussed, nor the existence of objects as partial intelligibilities wholly intelligible in him, multiple subsumptions of one simple intelligibility, but the reference will be to our mind: and then the question will be about the reality of matter and how far anything is real in itself and not precisely as held in mind and how ultimate reality is not purely formal and ideal.

This observation however comes to warn how easy is the slip from idealism into subjectivism. All idealists do not remain platonists, nor continue with Bishop Berkeley to hold that we are minds in a manifold world of intelligences held in the supreme intelligence of God, or that we are in a world of thoughts, though we are not the thinker. Having displaced the doctrine of indirect realism, this idealism in its turn bred, legitimately or otherwise, the doctrine that the object of our knowledge has an inner relationship to our mind, and this relationship modifies the object, and for all we know constitutes it. After that it is small help to assert that our thoughts must have come from somewhere else, for, as far as we know, there is no somewhere else: and when we say 'somewhere else' all that we are doing is to start off another series of thoughts. The attempt to strike an equation of the mental with the real, a comparison of the copy with the original, is an empty effort from the beginning, for an original is unthinkable. All we may hope to achieve is inner coherence, and then all we shall have done will be to have related our own mental forms with one another and to have eliminated those that seemed unnecessary or untidy.

But ideas must be caused, it may still be urged, for they are finite and not self-explicatory, even when considered as purely interior events. We have no experience of auto-causation, except for free-will, but that does not lie very deep.

This, however, does not prove that the cause of ideas is outside me, but merely that the cause is not the reasoning reason in the state selected for consideration. It may lie in another series of my thoughts, or, as some of the great idealists have held, in an absolute self within. Apart from this, we cannot lawfully invoke causality until we have satisfied ourselves that there is an existing world. Mental implication is one principle, real causality another; using causality to prove reality is like putting the cart before the horse.

Merely from an analysis of notions all we can know of causality is that it is a mental category. Some concepts imply others. From mental categories real existents cannot be inferred, and so we are still enclosed in the circle, though we may attempt to break out by the back door of materialism or of appetite; the materialism of forgetting our doubts in an enthralling adjustment of instruments and measurements, the appetite of resolving sickly doubts in a spasm.

But may not the circle be of our own making? Let us re-examine the possibility of a direct yet critical realism, which, having never admitted the radical dualism of thoughts and things and yet having allowed for the conceptual character of rational knowledge, denies that all knowledge is directed at such representations and affirms that at the base of knowledge we find ourselves confronted immediately with the real.

I look round my cabin. I formulate the idea of cabin, wishing that mine had been fitted out by a private firm, not by His Majesty's Dockyard. Underlying the comparisons and regrets I have fixed in my mind that a cabin is a living or sleeping enclosed space in a ship. And this definition is always issuing from and returning to an empirically observed situation in which I am one contestant. A perception of this or that is presupposed to all my cogitations, not as a postulate or arbitrary statement but as an opponent. Henceforward my thinking is not just an analysis of my interior noises and words: I may go off into reflections but always I return to the conviction that something is opposed to me, not necessarily in any inimical sense.

Primitively there is an *other*: we may call it the *suppositum*. The tension between subject and object is part of the foundation on which the tiers of our later knowledge are erected. The schematic constructions of the reasoning reason are purely logical modes unless this be supposed. The opposite object is an immediate datum, it is in the first place a *suppositum* without a predicate, not a form that has been reasoned out; and it is antecedent to reflection.

It is not pure being, for from that union would issue an act of

knowledge not unlike the beatific vision. God alone possesses sub-
sistent being with no thinking about it, no intervention of a
species. No, it is our experience of some thing that belongs to
being, a limited being, a partial being uttered and made by unlimited being. The experience bears on the thing, not on the
representation which immediately arises; there is an original perception of the real not-me: given to me, not fabricated by me.

It is a concrete thing, but need not be conceived as a solid
object existing independently of me in time and space. Space
may well be a mental category by which I locate my straying
experiences, an arrangement within a whole of parts, and time
another mental category, a succession of parts. But these are later
and more specialist questions, properly speaking they do not
belong entirely to epistemology or even to general metaphysics
but take us into natural philosophy. The other may fit in with the
picture painted by ordinary European commonsense or it may be
more wraithlike, but this is of no immediate consequence. What
does matter is that it is independent of our mind.

To strip our images and concepts down to the original metaphysical object is difficult, and to peel off the layers that we have
acquired from habits, memories, sensations, emotions, associa-
tions, but at the centre will be found this datum. Let it be called
being or thing without qualification. That lamp there, is it really
two feet from my typewriter? Is the Mediterranean a great
inland sea and are we afloat on it somewhere between the western
tip of Sicily and Cape Bon? The topic we are considering is
anterior to such questions. At its base my knowledge is an attempt
to express to myself the presence of a being or beings, independent
of and pre-existing to my thinking. It swiftly becomes an attempt
to translate them into rational forms congenial to my reason, and
so partly to possess them or be possessed by them, as a preface to
my entire union with the source of reality. The original knowledge is not of a representation but of what a representation
represents; not of reality at its source, but of some derivative
reality, for we would avoid the ontologism of saying that this
being is the very being of God, though at once beckoning to him.

So we are taken past and behind the *cogito*, for reflection does
not begin the process of thought, nor thought begin the process of
knowledge. If we refer to empirical observation it does not

appear that we start by thinking about our thinking as a purely subjective state whence we may or may not infer an objective reality. At the level of simple experience a simpler state of affairs is revealed. We are not aware at first of a duality between subject and object, nor of the internality of our thinking, but rather of objectivity, of a thing; then comes the curl back—of a thing other than us. The sentiment may or may not be an illusion, but it appears to be the first psychological stage of consciousness. What first is subjectively felt is not so much *I think* as *I know*. This is a less sophisticated reading of the original transaction, and therefore to be preferred.

What does it mean: *I know?* I know that something is. In the least committed sense it is tantamount to the principle of the affirmation of being. The mind, then, bears first on the *is* of being, not on the self. Then afterwards, as it sorts out the evidence for many things through the activity of its own internal senses, it accommodates itself to a sub-metaphysical world and arranges to live in a humane and scientific society.

When a mentalist protests, first that the primitive datum is present to consciousness and is a creature of consciousness, the premiss may be granted but the inference denied. The metaphysics of relations does not demand that a thing is really modified by a relationship to mind. Furthermore the psychological evidence shows that the object appears as something opposed to my consciousness. If one of the two is changed—not that this is necessary—it will be the knowing subject, not the object known.

Secondly to his argument that an object is known only in so far as it appears as a mental term, and therefore cannot be claimed to enjoy an independent existence, it can be replied that at the beginning the object is not a mental term but the subject of a mental term. Moreover the kantian order may be reversed, the necessity comes from it, not from me. In my heart I know I am as contingent as anything in my environment; hence the desire, at moments, to lose particular consciousness and sink again into the surrounding necessity.

Here are two characteristics, one of confronting me, the other of confronting me with indifference. Though at first they are but straws in the psychological wind they tell against a philosophy of subjectivism.

I

We may take it for granted that truth is primarily an affair of the mind, but we are not thereby mentalists. That an object exists mentally when I know it and that I know it only when it exists mentally does not affect the question of an independent *physical* existence one way or the other, and certainly does not decide the issue between realism and subjectivist idealism, any more than the fact that I can read French affects the fact that you may be able to read Lithuanian. The truism that we can know the characteristics only of the objects we know does not imply that the objects we do not know have no characteristics, still less that they are without existence.

By judicious questioning it seems that a subjectivist can be forced back to admit some objective standard; this may be clearer after we have discussed the field of criticism in the next chapter. An attitude of apologetic inferiority can be foisted on the intelligent by the learned, nevertheless plain ordinary realists may be comforted by the counter-attack on mentalism that has been launched by a combative realist philosophy of science.

The neo-realists have pointed out that to insist that everything when known is a form in consciousness is either to labour the obvious or to beg the question. Of course it is a condition of an object in consciousness to be a form in consciousness, but that the object is itself a purely mental entity, that is precisely the point under discussion.

Then they have named a formidable list of fallacies into which the unwary idealist is supposed to lapse. For instance when he argues that an idea cannot be mental and non-mental at the same time he falls into the argument of exclusive particularity, as if one were to say, 'Oh Disraeli was a statesman, you must be mistaken if you think he was a novelist.' Or into the fallacy of definition by initial predication, similar to what Mill called the fallacy of simple inspection, as if one were to argue; 'Blücher, why yes, boots; a cobbler, presumably; certainly not a field-marshal.'

Secondly, there is the fallacy of constantly shifting the point. For if, as most mentalists hold, the relationship of an object to mind is conceived of as a special entity in itself, and if a thing is real only because it is the object of a perception, then the perception itself is real only because it is the object of another perception, and this in its turn is real for the same reason, and so on and so on indefinitely, which to say the least is an embarrassing state of affairs for a scientist who is working to a goal.

We may move out of the problem of knowledge for a moment and note the impossibility of an infinite regress in finding evidence: if in working back there were no ultimate reason which itself is not a conclusion to another truth, there would never be in working forward any arresting conclusion, for what never starts at an explanation can never stop at one.

This is not to say that an infinite series of individual events merely contingently connected with one another is impossible. There seems to be nothing repugnant in pure thought to the assembly of an infinite multitude, though the housing difficulties in a physical universe may be decisively unfavourable and the members may not be able to be present all at once. But an infinite series of terms in essential subordination is impossible. When I type a full stop, and then seek to explain it causally, so far as philosophy is concerned it may be the last of a series of full stops stretching back endlessly, and the typewriter may be a perpetual typewriter that never began to exist, in the sense of emerging once upon a time from the metal. But whether perpetual or temporary the machine, and whether the stop be the fifty-thousandth or one that cannot be numbered because it belongs to a series that never had a first, I am as far off as ever from giving a reason for it, and am compelled as much as ever, if I am to explain the situation, to go out of the causal series of typewriters into the higher series of manual acts and motive commands of intelligence. Infinite horizontal prolongation does not dispense with the need for a limited vertical rise.

Thirdly the neo-realists thrust the argument for subjectivism into a confused indentification of a truism and an absurdity: the flat platitude—we can know only those objects present to our mind when they are known; and the inconsequence—we know that the objects can exist only when they are known. And when the argument is stated as follows: an idea is incapable of existing apart from mind, but a known entity is an idea, therefore a known entity is incapable of existing apart from mind—the term *idea* has two different senses and the argument labours in equivo-cation. For in the major premiss *idea* signifies a mental process or state, while in the minor premiss it signifies an object of thought.

To slip from one to the other is like identifying feeling *cold* and *feeling* cold, an identification of a state of sensibility with an object of sensibility, which to quote a neo-realist reproach in order to close on a resounding phrase, is the verbal fallacy of psychophysical metonymy.

These logomachies may now be left on one side as we pause over the prelogical presence of a real object to the reason. We return to the question, How is it present? Examination will show that the inquiry has shifted from epistemology to philosophical psychology. The discussion about two things so interacting and mutually possessing one another without suffering any loss then hinges on the nature and the types of movement, and should be conducted according to the temper if not the terms of Aristotle on the *Physics* and on the *Soul*.

Let us suppose that several people are looking at what we agree to call a tree. There are as many phenomenal appearances as there are people, possibly many more if they look at it long enough; all are different representations, are differently pitched, have different ambiguities and echoes, carry different emotional charges. But deepest is the level of meaning, and there all may agree. Having agreed to make an abstraction, we find ourselves with one and the same tree. Stripped from everything personal and peculiar to the onlookers the bare judgement remains: a tree is a perennial plant with a single self-supporting trunk. Now we come to a being and a meaning common to all concerned, approaching a vague but pervasive object that is above criticism, an object underlying all our appreciation of the pinewoods at Ravenna, the giant sequoia, and the mulberry we have planted in the garden. When we get down to this skeleton tree we have forgotten alike the subjectivist to whom objects are just flickers of a mind and the realist to whom they are concrete slabs of duration.

The critical interest, as we shall see, lies more on the surface and rises when all the parties concerned judge what they are looking at to be in fact a tree. It represents the fifth period of philosophical realism, and here critical philosophy manifestly comes into its own. Before touching on this let us remind ourselves that scientific philosophy is no more than a patch within the wider frontier of reality; a very large patch it is true, conterminous with every rational human interest, and one that we are obliged to cultivate. But what the scholastics would call the material object of man's activity is very much bigger. All truth is not reasoned truth, all good is not an object of choice. The formal object of man's scientific activity, including his high scientific activity or philosophy, is the translation of that wide reality into his rational pattern, rational in the narrowest application to discursive and consequential knowledge, not in the widest sense of intelligence and vision. God is not a metaphysician, and men will surpass science. Metaphysics may still survive, a necessity in hell, but an idle luxury in heaven.

Chapter VII
THE FIELD OF CRITICISM

FROM the premisses we have laid out we can infer that the discernment of what is true from what is false is a special and not a general problem. In other words the issue cannot be pressed to the most universal terms, for there is no positive contradictory to being. Nought but nothingness opposes being as such. Consequently there is some truth in every statement however improbable, just as there is some good in every choice however perverse. The covering may be bizarre, the consequences disastrous, but there is always something at the heart of the activity, otherwise it would be sheerly negative and just not there at all. The atheist is protesting against the travesty of God presented to his mind, the sinner at bottom proves, not that there is evil in his heart, but that there are too many goods in the world.

The contrast of true and false represents an opposition of particular forms in material logic. So does the contrast of right and wrong in moral philosophy. It is this opposition that now must be taken into a more living and dialectical contrast. Things comes to us fleshly, said Luther, and we make them ghostly. It is in the judgements of the spirit that the problem is stated. The world is a stubborn rock, but we make it a shadow; it could be a revelation, but we make it a deceit.

34. Composition of Scene

Let us pretend that we are all the victims of a gigantic hoax. We are set in a world where the sovereign and deceiving intelligence of the Prince of Darkness has so contrived that the appearances of things in our minds are utterly unlike their realities. This nightmare of Descartes is haunting only if we are indirect realists who believe that our ideas are the objects of our knowledge and that their correspondence with things has to be proved and this might, but for a benevolent providence, have a twisted spell laid on it. If however we are direct realists the trance, for all its

118

queerness, could not affect our fundamental perception of being, but only the interpretations and constructions we work out from our experience. The nightmare would render impossible the sober and systematic account of the world, such as we are accustomed to expect from natural science, but mathematics is untouched and in theory at any rate, metaphysics could manage almost as well as now, and perhaps better, for it could proceed undisturbed by genial substitutes.

In a sense the critical philosopher can echo the Autocrat of the Breakfast-Table: 'Give us the luxuries of life, and we will dispense with its necessaries.' The function of critical science is to separate the true from the false on the basis of something given. It cannot admit an ultimate doubt. Error, says St Thomas, is not the simple negation of truth, but its contrary privation; it is in a subject and involves a truth, just as blindness is only attributed to him who should be able to see. Criticism deals with the elaborations of knowledge, many of which will have to be questioned and some of them rejected on further examination. In so doing it will turn back to what is already possessed or seems to be possessed, but there comes a moment when doubt is merely methodic and the mind is quizzical rather than profoundly dubious. The suspense is induced in order that we can see what happens when we argue as if a conviction were not true. Such a critical method is based on realism and is quite different from the doubt of mentalism, which begins with a hesitation that we discover too late cannot be superseded in theory; the doubt becomes negative and we have nothing to go on.

The element in knowledge originally independent of reasoning should not be pictured as totally non-mental. Surds to lower levels of consciousness may be solved in a higher; matter opaque to the human mind may be lucid to a spiritual intelligence. Neither should the play of the mind in the first presentation of its object be suppressed. The mind is not a passive principle subject to reaction, like a photographic film impressed with the image of a scene. Because independent of a mind, it does not follow that an object is strange and in another order, or that the subject and the object do not interpenetrate. A distinction is drawn between action that works to produce an exterior effect and activity in which two terms are engaged but lie within one another. All

knowledge, in varying degrees, belongs to this second class. The
entrance of the mind into its object does not constitute an entity
which is itself the object of knowledge or a relation that is a
positive and real addition to its subject; its operations resemble
those of enzymes in the production of organic energy.

Three moments can be distinguished, of the thing as thing,
of the thing as a mental object, of the thing expressed as a thought.
The pause between the first and the second is the one that counts
in the present question; yet all three are in and of the same stuff;
they are three points that should be taken in a successive but continuous flow. Though for purposes of epistemological and psychological criticism they can be isolated, the process itself should not
be picked to pieces.

The innocent pride of the morning—no error arises in the
first intercourse, and for that matter no fully developed truth
either: St Thomas often limits truth and error to the later judgements we make about things. And even here, as Donne writes,

> though truth and error bee
> Neare twins, yet truth a little elder is.

For as evil of its nature cannot be fundamental, since the existence
of a good subject and a deficient reference to a good end within
the general finality of good are supposed, so neither can falseness,
which supposes a subject capable of truth but mistaken with a
misconstruction within the general operation plan of evidence.
Error affects us only when we begin to elaborate, just as wrong
affects us only when we make a decision. But as the human will
reaches adult statute for good or ill in a choice, so also the human
reason finds itself for true or false when it becomes itself, that is
not just a recipient of information but a maker of judgements,
not a patient but an agent.

But the start of our knowledge is too deep for doubt, and to
this extent is beyond criticism. An ultimate doubt elicits a false
question, a question, moreover, that cannot even be properly
phrased. The scholastics knew that unanswerable questions were
unreasonable, and this gives them a solidity, because they sought
no impossible reassurance. It also partly explains their silence on
the epistemological problem, though in critical company a hundred years ago this would have been like that doubtful compli-

ment made by Sydney Smith; 'it was the occasional flashes of silence that made Macaulay's conversation delightful.'

Error is possible only in a judgement, and then only in special and derived types of judgement, namely, in an insociable combination of notes, as in the conclusion to the limerick:

> She went off one day
> In a relative way,
> And came back the previous night.

or in the misapplication of a predicate to an existent, as when it is said that the sun really grows bigger as it sets to the west. But an impossible association does not invalidate the elements or a misapplication the subject of the mistake. This is not the place to discuss illusions, hallucinations, mistaken identities, and other forms of deception, except to remark that examination will show them to be examples of compound knowledge, and therefore not militating against the original simplicities. The tests for truth to be applied to developed and argued forms of knowledge cannot be too exacting, but a critique is not bound to adopt a sincere universal doubt of all principles, indeed it cannot, for a positive doubt must have a reason.

No power can deny itself, for no natural impulse is suicidal; even biological surrenders have a positive purpose. One can be thwarted by another, it is true, but what other power is there to controvert the mind, not by force, but by evidence? Not appetite, for that is unnamed until adopted by mind, and is unable to question the intelligibility which alone gives it human value. Naughtiness may do for a spree, but not for a life. Perversion will not stay a civilization. However fantastic the logic in which we may move our thoughts and however remote we make them from their ordinary meanings, some real relations are always presupposed. There is a categoric knowledge of being which is unaffected though we stand on our heads and squint with one eye.

35. *As If*

If so desired a quasi-universal doubt may be adopted temporarily as an expedient. Sometimes a truth is made clearer by a *per impossibile* argument and confirmed by the spectacle of the results that would follow were it not true; a food specialist might arrange for a patient to go without fruit and fresh vegetables in order to study the onset of scurvy. Did reality not exist it would be necessary to invent it, if only to explain how the mind is always hankering after the inexpugnable *is*.

The line of critical doubt may be developed with interest, but finally a stage is reached when it rests on a complete fiction. To prolong a real universal doubt to the very end would be more extravagant than decapitation to cure a toothache: that at least does something. The premisses of any particular system or habit of thought may be decanted from our minds; we are still left with *is*. Of such radical criticism it may be said that while the language grows more refined the thought may coarsen, for the process tends to solidify what should be flowing and to separate and make little particles of modes and relations that should merge wholly in the complete situation and be entirely open. Thus direct realism may be lissomer and less lumpy than indirect realism; an intellectual poet moves more in one piece than does a reflective poet: Donne is more disencumbered and less embarrassing than Patmore.

Epistemology is not a science distinct from and antecedent to metaphysics; still less is metaphysics merely a corollary to epistemology. The latter is not a self-contained enquiry, complete with its own proper principles and its own peculiar evidence. By and large it is just metaphysics become self-regarding and to that extent self-critical; not mistrusting itself so much as turning back to scrutinize the premisses. This must be done before there can be a reasoned elaboration on the properties and consequences of being, a discussion of such questions as the nature of substance and of the four causes; it is as though the heavy oil of metaphysics needs a spark from the more volatile fuel of epistemology.

The problem of knowledge is subsumed in the general principle of being, and is set in a system of reference wider than that of detailed enquiries into the validity of various special types of knowledge. Such specialist criticism is bound up with scientific method and to that extent is part of natural philosophy. The critique of the sciences is, as it were, the material logic corresponding to the special sciences, and all of them have their own special epistemologies. The problem of knowledge in all its amplitude however belongs to nothing less than first and general philosophy.

Though valuable corroboration may be afforded, the attempt to establish a realist philosophy by the methods of physiology or of psychology does not itself reach beyond certain local ends. For the same reason, philosophical realism cannot be disproved by any special line of empirical research. Yet the condition of affairs is healthy when high philosophy confirms, and if necessary helps to rehabilitate the confidence of commonsense in the ordinary working postulates of the sciences. Prosczpina comes back from the lower world, and laughing Ceres reassumes the land. The cosmos, we should presume in advance, hangs together as one; it is ominous when specialists set themselves to open and widen the fissures. Intercourse should be vigorous and straightforward; it bodes ill when speculation becomes fine spun and artificial. The results of reflection should not be dissociated from straight experience, otherwise we run the risk of philosophizing fragmentarily and intermittently and of apologizing for being ordinarily human.

On the other hand the works of philosophy cannot be reduced to the products of ordinary commonsense. The glorification of the metaphysical common man is an understandable reaction to the sophistication of the academics; it may be sometimes a growling and spluttery condemnation of what is novel and imperfectly appreciated, as when a blimp is confronted with a new movement in art. But the retreat of metaphysics to an earlier cultural simplicity is not to be recommended at a time when the sciences themselves have departed from the customary amenities of conversation. In any case philosophy has little to do with a middling sort of ideal.

Commonsense, however, implies a rudimentary and initial metaphysics, a concrete manifestation of the habit of fundamental principles, weightily rather than scientifically stated. Two extremes have to be avoided; on one hand boorishness before the delicacies of thought, and on the other, archness far removed from the raciness of idiomatic knowledge. Commonsense usually takes any respectable epistemological object as an ontological object as well, respectable, that is when supported by a convergence of evidence from different quarters and when it appears both practical and advantageous.

At the bottom of thought is that which is. Up to a point common agreement is a fair enough test; acting on that as if it were right we shall not go far wrong. At least we shall be in step with other members of the community. There is some basis in reality even for the common illusions, old wives's tales, and strange conventions whose strangeness passes unnoticed because they are so usual. Why should we shake hands? Yet underneath many of them lies an unmitigated experience of the grandeur and misery of birth and death, sex and war. Mind and heart beat in tune with reality when the *in memoriam* notices of a provincial newspaper can be read with pity and without patronage.

Nevertheless all the common affirmations of humanity cannot be cast in the same mould. Minds are not obedient to the exact laws according to which water starts to freeze at the same temperature and all plane trees rustle in the same way and all shingle beaches take the same pattern from the tides. A truthful mind is not a subject receiving a mechanical impression and copy and acting in accordance with the fixed laws of physics. There may be exact agreement about logic and ideal significance, but existence rings at a different pitch in every mind. Being is analogical, and within itself now more, now less.

36. *The Physical-Mental*

The apparatus of knowing is altogether more subtle, though it is really not a piece of mechanism at all, not even the most delicate, such as a photo-electric cell. Knowing is a function of nature, yet unlike other functions in that it ranges freely and enters into the life of other things without changing them or losing itself. Most physical actions are spent in producing a change; energy can be imagined streaming out from the cause, and a system of causes and effects can be pictured as an engine made up of different parts in reciprocating motion. For the processes of knowledge, however, we should have to imagine elements merging into one another and yet preserving their separateness, washing round one another and entering and pervading, like the shadow fronds in a rock-pool, mingling and disengaging in the green reflections.

The immanent motions of life cannot be exhibited as mechanical movements, still less do the highest motions of life in consciousness conform to the categories of physical causation. The postulate of a double existence on the part of the object known has already been referred to, the first is the physical being of a thing unstated in human consciousness, the second is the investing mental being taken on in human consciousness. Now these two, the *natural* and the *intentional*, should not be represented as separate and distinct entities or things. The imagination fails us here because of its tendency to solidify and make concrete the images it forms: they are credited with a present substance, their expectations and relations are scarce hinted at. Yet the *intentional being* is wholly relative to the subject knowing and the object known, particularly to the latter. As a sign it is entirely derivative from and anticipatory of something else. As a reality, of course, it is a quality of the subject knowing, but its content of meaning is a gesture outwards.

As such then it should not be represented as a thing in itself, even though it be a counterpart of something else. In looking at a tree, real modifications take place in the beholders, real qualities that are more like a tree than are the impressions they receive from staring at a locomotive. But the significant form is not these physiological and psychological qualities; the relative content of the perceptions cannot be reduced to the physical elements, just as the meaning for me of a photograph cannot be taken down to the emulsion or even to the light and shade and shape resemblance between the original scene and the copy. The relative form, then, should be clearly distinguished from the physical substratum in which it is set: it is not a physical entity at all in the sense of being a quantity or a quality, it does not correspond to the object as one thing to another thing; it is entirely *sui generis*; it is a relation.

From one angle it is the object as known, from another the subject as knowing. For in knowledge there is an incomparable union between mind and object. Even to the lowest, the least, the most transient, Aristotle's dictum in some measure applies, that the knower becomes the known. There is an identification rather than a correspondence. For correspondence implies two differently realities of the same order matching one another: a word in one language may correspond to a word in another, but a word is said to correspond to an idea, not because of its physical

characteristics, its pronunciation or look on a page, but because
of its significance. Relations are not intermediate things between
the relatives; motherhood should not come between mother and
child.

The union in knowledge is at once more rarified and more
intimate than any other union in nature. More rarified in that
the subject does not necessarily get a kick from the object, for
cognition itself requires neither an organic impression in the subject nor a real change in the object; more intimate in that the form
of another is possessed. For though as a psychological quality of
the subject an idea may be distinct from the object, as a meaning
it is identical. Physiological changes are present in sensation,
and the action and passion of causality accompany human reasoning, but knowledge as such is a relationship without previous becoming, without dominance on one side and subjection on the
other, though we might never have appreciated this but for the
theology of the Trinity.

In such a description of knowledge the measures of location
are secondary. We do not have to decide whether my mind is
here and the object is there by pointing to different positions in
space. Originally and before the emergence of clear notions there
is a perception of being; not until later is individual consciousness
separated from the general community. And not until then, after
we have stood back, as it were, and held things at arm's length,
does the problem of doubt arise in the intellectual order. Similarly
in the moral order the problem of guilt does not arise until the
sense of estrangement.

We feel ourselves to be embodied in particular matter, and
then proceed to deal with different things, which we take to
occupy different positions outside our body. Thing is separated
from thing, and things from our thoughts about them. Yet the
distinction should be deft, and the terms should not be moved
about as so many solid and separable things, like pieces of money,
especially when the terms refer to ideas. For if they are treated
as different pieces, or even as different parts of the same subject,
they are easily pictured as things in their own right, and the mind
is confronted again with the impasse at the end of indirect
realism. Reality lurks obscurely behind the ideas and presently is
dispensed with altogether.

The trouble is of our own making, and once landed in it we are constrained either to show that ideas are mirrors of reality or that they are counters in our mind corresponding to things outside. We may try to do this by complicated map readings and calculations. But we should do better to look simply to the lie of the land. A concept is merely a sign, and should be swept immediately to what is signified, and this swiftly is more than an essence, it is a thing. For though a definition does not imply the existence of what is defined, an existential stress is laid on the origin of every complete judgement. The first idea in the mind is not a purely notional meaning, an *ens rationis*, for this is a second thought, to be referred back at once to a first reading. This first reading is an induction or abstraction from a primitive and concrete real intelligibility.

When they are considered as qualities, logical notions are of course as real as any other perception or affection, though not so intense. If we possessed a psychological X-ray apparatus we should observe how the mind is as encrusted with concepts of logical entities as with concepts of real entities. It is as relative and significant forms that they differ, for the latter are immediately related to a world transcending our consciousness.

37. *Criticism of Judgement*

The tests for truth and error lie in the second of the three stages of mental activity, apprehension, judgement, reasoning. Apprehension is the assembly point, but the movement to truth or error is not yet under way; and the crisis has come before reasoning develops, though there are special logical fallacies attending the process. It may go off on a wild-goose chase, but the first issue for criticism rises at the stage of judgement.

Apprehension is the simple confrontation of the mind with an object and the utterance of an unattached meaning; and though an incongruous idea may be formed, or rather an incongruous composition of ideas—rational quadruped is the example given by St Thomas—this does not amount to a full-blown error. At this stage the two aspects of incident and meaning can be distinguished. There is the perception of an event, vivid or dull as the case may be, the reaction to a phenomenon, visible, audible, smelly, tactile, or a compound of sensible stimuli; there is moreover the understanding of a general meaning not bound up with any one sense impression in space and time. The distinction lies between image and idea: yet so long as neither carries an affirmation or a negation they are neither truthful nor false. The child exclaims, 'Moo-cow!' *moo*, that is the image, *cow*, that verges on the idea, for a type is expressed that is applied to more than one image, a unity of meaning is associated with a variety of sense impressions.

The mere evocation of a meaning, however, is not liable to criticism. It is neither true nor false; in isolation from the context and until framed in a judgement there is little to be said in reply. The child might just as well have cried *swallow* or *book* or *Abyssinian maid and upon her dulcimer she played*. But the child indicates, 'Look, moo-cow,' wishing to share its knowledge and pointing to a fact, and it is then when we proceed to pass judgements, and we begin very early, that the categories true and false can be applied. 'Look, nanny, there's a moo-cow.'—'No, pet, it's a bull.'

The elements of knowledge, therefore, are not called in question just because their composition is mistaken. A star may be still seen an astronomical number of years after extinction: the sight is not mistaken but the judgement is, if it affirms that the star is still shining millions of miles away. In much the same way sensations may be mistaken when some kind of sense-judgement is made, as when a bear blunders by climbing a telegraph pole because the humming of the wires has been mistaken for a hive of honey-bees.

The difference between our dreams and waking thoughts lies in the character of the statements we make. In both cases the elements are very much the same; in the former they freely associate and combine without discipline, in the latter they are attributed to an existent world. Are dreams truly representative? The material that is shaped is no less real than the stuff of our waking consciousness, and perhaps some people may feel that their compositions in sleep are better authentications of reality than the systems they adopt when they are awake—'and we in dreams behold the Hebrides.' To say that dreams are fantastic is no condemnation. But when we say of anyone, of Balzac for instance, that in his life real facts were not discerned from the creatures of his fancy, then adverse criticism may begin.

Objects are perceived and a composition of scene is stated in well-founded judgements and illusions alike. But whereas in the former case there is corroboration from a great deal of other evidence, in the latter case the impression is judged to be out of harmony with nearly everything else we know. Yet so long as a mere fancy remains unasseverating it is as free from error as an Emmet railway.

A mistake is always a misjudgement. The problem of knowledge does not enter so long as objects are represented merely as meanings to the mind. But when such epistemological objects are made ontological by being referred to an existent, then criticism begins, and we may ask whether the convenient compression of speech, 'I see a cow' means anything more than 'I see the image of a cow,' or, 'I have the impression that I am seeing a cow.'

Doubt follows because a judgement has been ventured. The mind has left its enclosure and now finds itself exposed to the danger of error. A split has been made in the content of knowledge: this/is/cow. Knowledge has been articulated. The self has separated itself from its environment by saying, 'that there,' and in that environment has proceeded to separate the *is* and the *what* by affirming an existent and indicating its nature.

It is here that criticism should be applied, and not before. The mind has a knife, but it is surgical not lethal. For though judgements and elaborations may be erroneous and dissection is needed, however drastically this may operate, the first elements always remain beyond criticism. It is as though we can always pull down a house, but cannot escape the necessity of working from the same quarry and sandpit and woodland.

St Thomas adopts the saying of Aristotle that understanding is always true, in other words that the original reaction cannot be questioned. In explanation he quotes St Augustine, anyone who is in error does not understand that about which he is in error; in other words, the first impression is wrongly interpreted and elaborated and applied. He draws a comparison with sensation. A sense is not deceived about its proper and peculiar object, which responds to its primary and natural impulse, unless for extraneous reasons of damage or disease. But with regard to common and mixed objects, sensations can be wrongly worked up, as when we assess the size or shape of objects or imagine that we see a blue moon.

K

Mistakes are easier still with inferential objects, as when a poison-ous species is mistaken for an edible fungus.

Error affects the sense of context and general situation. Now the first clear object of reason is a simple meaning of a thing, and here the mind makes no mistake. It is when we take our bearings from this perception that blunders are made, as when the mind sets one thing in relation to other things, either by passing nega-tive or positive judgements or by reasoning. Incidentally error here may recoil on an initial apprehension when it becomes an interpretation of a fact, as when a dolphin is mistaken for a mer-maid, or when impossible or improbable mixtures are conceived, such as a virtuous lie or a rational bird.

Truth is the conformity of mind and thing, and hence, says St Thomas, to know truth is to know this conformity. Human theoretic truth is the conformity of our mind with a thing, and to know this conformity demands reflexion. The ability to reflect is beyond both the power of sense and the function of understand-ing a simple meaning. Only in judging that a thing exists as it is known does the mind commit itself to a truth or falsehood as the case may be. When they are working healthily truth exists in the senses and intellectual apprehension, but this does not amount to the truth as known in knower. The complete meaning of truth requires such a conscious reflexion, and so does full-blown human error, just as perfect sin demands deliberation. Things and simple reactions do not come to decisions. Though they are objects of scientific truthfulness, the truthfulness does not lie in them but in the judgements we make about them.

'Damn you, sir, don't stand there pawing the air, put your hands in your pockets,' said George IV to Robert Peel. 'Damn you, sir,' was the testy answer, 'I have no pockets.' The story applies to critical philosophy, for mentalism suffers from the same handicap. The mind must strike an attitude before it can be criticized. And then, if it is to carry off the interview with non-chalance and a corinthian calm, it must have pockets.

CHAPTER VIII

POSSIBLE THEREFORE REAL

'A FINE fellow; but too stoical for my taste,' said Macaulay about Romilly. 'I love a little of the Epicurean element in virtue.' A similar chill may be felt about the abstractions of philosophy. Nevertheless they should be sustained a little longer, if we are to give the ordinary human affections a metaphysical status and eventually recover richness. We have looked behind the first layer of human experience, behind colour and sound and scent; we have left on one side the individual characteristics in our perception, the difference between the feel of a Saturday afternoon and a Monday morning: furthermore we are neglecting the general physical properties, unconcerned with the difference between chalk and cheese and with the moving sensibility of material objects; we have gone past their figuration in a mathematical scheme and are attempting to take *isness* stripped.

Then comes the compulsion of judging that being is being, being is not non-being, non-being is not being. The principles of identity and contradiction stiffen the skeleton of reasoned thought, by which our consciousness is separated from confusion, and but for which it might melt into its surroundings. The opposition between being and non-being is more profound and decisive than any duel in the myths. For to the philosopher nothingness is not even chaos, for that at least is a disorder and a tumult of things, but the complete blank of impossibility, the void of sheer unthinkableness, the blind before the pretences of square circles and virtuous betrayals and contradictories claiming simultaneous truth.

The mind cannot stretch to nothingness, nor the appetite to hunger. Being is what can be known, as food is what can be salutarily eaten. Pure nothingness cannot be an object of mind. By accepting this concept of being as object of mind, it is submitted, we are quickly committed to an existing reality, and that without unlawful smuggling of formal meanings into the realm of extra-rational things. Philosophy perhaps too easily may resign itself to a set of ideal essences; its habits of formal analysis encourage the persuasion. Some philosophers seem well content to stay there; others, haunted by the need of making existential affirmations, look to a historical religion to supplement their philosophy; others by the same token invoke literature or the vivid experience of living. Without discounting the need for such complements, let us pause to see whether science at its most austere does not warm to existence.

38. *Mere Thoughts*

On inspection mental objects appear to fall into two classes. Some present the character of complete dependence on a reasoning mind such as ours, others claim more independence. While the *genus of roses* is regarded as more or less real, and the *human species* too, and the *conclusion come to by Allenby* to launch his cavalry across the Plain of Esdraelon is held to have been a historic and momentous event, *genus as such*, or *species as such*, or *conclusion as such* are not accounted to have an existence outside our minds. We do not expect to meet them wandering abroad, they are merely thoughts about thoughts. So also a host of other mental objects, such as class, consequence, middle term of a syllogism, priority, and so forth.

They are examples of *ens rationis*, logical being, a fiction we make up for ourselves as a mental convenience, an object limited to the human mind and found nowhere else, for a higher mind is not argumentative and presumably has no use for such categories. They are part of the pattern we weave to give our ideas a scientific dress. They are second thoughts to our first thoughts; called by the scholastics, entities of the second intention. What truth they have is wholly subservient to the demands of logic. Were they to remain with them, philosophers would be like those dead-letter legalists who wrote commentaries on commentaries, the academic jurists of the medieval complaint, *non glossant glossas, sed glossarum glossas*.

Nevertheless logical entities are not counterfeits of things nor are they devoid of all real meaning. They are artefacts, but not cerebral caprices. They are contrivances without which the reason cannot scientifically systematize its other knowledge or shape its thoughts about reality. What they contain is formally subjective and mental, but not wholly baseless. Even purely logical judgements imply existential affirmations.

In this logical setting of consciousness the contradictory and the sheerly impossible may be invested with fictional substance by a kind of sleight of mind, which having held up a being then proceeds to remove coherence from it. Take away what you first thought of. Though unable to exist in reality, sheer nothingness may be pinned down as a logical term and credited with an equivalent existence. This can be done by thinking of *being* and then setting the general concept in one-sided reference to its opposite. So is formed the idea of what is contradictory or nothing, both of them authentic terms in argument. Total nothingness is much more vacuous than the absence of created being that can be imagined to precede creation considered as a production that once upon a time began. For then there was not a complete blank, otherwise nothing would ever have begun. A reference to the eternal intelligibility of things in the divine mind and to almighty power is always implicit.

Complete nothingness is also more absolute than the relative nothingness involved in any being less than the infinite being. Relative or creaturely nothingness is the absence of this or that kind of being; in this sense any limited thing may be written down by a fiction as a compound of being and non-being. But total nothingness indicates a term that cannot be transmuted into reality, the non-entity devoid of intelligibility and attraction. The step from nothing to being is purely logical. The first term is a logical entity inasmuch as we can find a term for it and deal with it in debate, though perhaps all that we are doing is to make a conversational nod in its direction, like the politer authors on spiritual deportment when confronted with the beastlier manifestations of human nature.

At periods the reason shows a fondness for the irrational, even in preference to the supra-rational; perhaps because the rational is too smug, the supra-rational too grandiloquent. Yet even so it offers a tribute to reasonableness. However tangled and torn the fine-lacery of our thoughts, there is no destroying the reasonable texture entirely. There is no contradiction that has no grain of sense; surrealism is not without significance; and, as the seventeenth-century divine exclaimed, 'Tho' we speak Nonsense, God will pick out the Meaning of it.'

These logical artefacts need be chased no farther: all are less real and at the same time more useful than chimeras; some are the ordinary accompaniments of consecutive and classifying thinking; others are fictive objects invented by the reason for its own convenience. Usually they are objects of the second intention, but indeed there are objects to the *n*th intention. I can think of the notion of my thinking, and then of the notion of the notion, and so on almost endlessly. I can think of ideas instead of things, and of words instead of ideas. Psychological introspection can go on without finish, one thought always chasing the tail of another. Prudence is needed to halt the series before it leads to madness.

Logic in like manner can pursue its own proper analyses, at least verbally. But our business is not with objects that are obviously not of our own making, but with those other ones that wear an air of greater independence. Whereas artificial objects are true by reference to the intention of the artist, *artifex non peccat volens*, these other ones appear to be less for our convenience and less under our control. Our ideas about them are true as forms, not of self-expression, but of respect for and conformity to a reality beyond us. Underlying every association of thoughts lies a basic judgement about existence.

39. *Beyond Logic*

Verum, says St Hilary, *est declarativum et manifestativum esse*: any truth declares existence. The study of mental forms as such is not the work of metaphysics, nor even of psychology, but of logic, which analyses their notional co-efficients and disposes them into correct and elegant patterns. These may be profitably studied as part of a commentary on our thinking, given intercourse with reality; otherwise they are merely a luxury, and unwholesome at that. They are preceded by first thoughts, objects of the first intention, *entia primae intensionis*.

These objects are taken, rightly or wrongly, to possess more than a mental existence in the reasoning faculty. They are differently toned from purely logical entities, and we allow them a different respect. When, for instance, we say that cruelty to children is horrible, cruelty and horror and children are supposed to be more real than predicates and subjects of sentences, which in fact they also are. In discussing these terms we do not think that we are dealing with a situation restricted to the field of logic. They rouse things, not merely objects that can be named.

Predicates and subjects and the rules of logical relevance are objects precisely as present to reasoning attention. Cruelty and horror are also objects in the same way, for they are abstract generalities that do not exist as such in the world. Who has even encountered naked cruelty or unabated horror? Yet there is a difference between them and logical entities. Though abstractions exist only in the mind—abstract liberty, says Burke, like other mere abstractions is not to be found—yet some of them lie close enough to our lives to move us. We may have witnessed a person acting cruelly and felt within ourselves the sentiment of horror—perhaps some Balkan thug taking it out of his opponent's family, an experience all the worse because the instruction of home authorities has forbidden intervention. Events affecting individual substances are what most people take as the prime realities. They have the kick of existence.

The first intentions of the reason, however, are less urgent and tangible. They result on withdrawal from the conditions and circumstances of historic existence when the mind contemplates forms more stylized and general, objects having a lesser intensity of being than have existing subjects, but real all the same, as when cruelty and horror are regarded apart from individual occurrences. Meanings are examined, which meanings are supposed to be fairly immediately applicable to existent things. In fact the application will determine whether a person is a man of principle or not.

They are rational meanings, but they are assumed to have a sharper turn to existence than is the case with logical notions. They are, as it were, at only one remove from reality, while logical notions are two or more removes away; they are ideas about things, not ideas about ideas. They appear to point, not to a mental and logical mode of existence, but to a condition apart from logic and reasoned consciousness.

These objects, lying midway between mere thoughts and brutal things, are the forms of philosophical science. Mere thoughts either make no gesture to reality or that gesture has to be construed, while as for things we are not certain yet that they exist. What the philosophical reason is confronted with are certain types, and it remains to be seen if the analysis of them discloses an existent outside the mind.

40. Possibles

Taking them in general we notice that real ideas fall into two classes. Some are reputedly actual; we say of them that they are; others are reputedly possible, we say of them that they could be. The former refer to objects we take to be existing or to have existed; man's cruelty to man, some men's aversion from cruelty. The latter refer to objects that could exist, a royalist movement in the United States, a Uniate Church of England, a geophysical slide resulting in a tropical climate for the Orkneys and Shetlands; there are degrees of possibility and such ideas range from the not-at-all-impossible to the highly-unlikely.

The present argument can afford to neglect ideas that claim to express actual existents, and can treat all our first ideas as hypothetical to existence, that is as expressing merely what is able to exist. We know the meaning of tree, but let us pretend that we are doubtful whether trees exist, or at most allow that they exist only in so far as they are seen. But notice, it is this reference to existence, whether or not fulfilled in fact, that stamps the difference between these possible objects and logical artefacts. By this they are different from the utterly impossible, and from merely logical transcriptions, and for the same reason.

> I have an aunt in Yucatan
> Who kept a python for a pet—

she is a figure in nonsense verse, and does not exist. But she could. A historical fiction, she is not thereby a logical figment, such as are the figures in 'Come in, said the Genus, make yourself at home with one of my little Species.'

This aunt is an example of a type of object that, first, may lead to the conclusion that some sciences are not just departments of logic, and secondly, that some sciences touch a reality independent of their purely ideal content. First, let us develop the implications of the statement that such or such an object is not impossible. It will be discovered that the first requirement of a possible is a coherence of composition, furthermore that it has the note of being able to be apart from the mind, though this ring of existence, so different from that of logic, will not be sounded until the next section.

We may think of examples from the radiant world of phantasy, Manon Lescaut or Betsy Prig, Falstaff or Jeeves, or more soberly keep to the world of things which might have existed or might yet exist, Prester John and ash-trees yet to grow in Breckland. The purest type of possible is that of which there are no premonitions in our environment, and with these we remain.

When we say that such or such a thing is possible, we usually go outside the notion itself to consult its surroundings. We conceive the object to be within the power of some principle to produce. It is possible that the convoy will get through to Murmansk if the weather is bad enough; it is possible that some of the ships will be sunk if we are engaged by Heinkels and U-boats. This throws us back to the possibility not so much of the effect as of the cause, an extrinsic principle on which the event depends. But this will not suffice, for we are seeking the root condition of being-able-to-be.

Moreover in judging that a thing is able to be by reference to an outside principle, both the effect and the cause are considered as different beings of a certain nature and of a definite kind, and so we are then committed to this and that sort of being, not with being in general. Also we are left to explain what makes the cause possible? But we are searching for a more general answer to a more general question: what constitutes the possibility of being and what do we touch at bottom when we say that an object is able to be, though we may be doubtful about its existence in an actual fact?

The first answer is that objects are possible when they manifest no interior contradiction, or, more positively, when they possess an inner coherence.

The full objects of rational attention are composite; they can be resolved into parts; not in the sense that they are like mosaic pavements or porcupines; or that they contain diverse quantitative parts, though probably they often will; nor even that they exhibit composition between a substantial and modal being or between different specific elements, though all these compositions will often occur. But always they will carry the distinction between *what* and *is*.

An act of complete rational knowledge is cast in the form of a judgement. The simplest example is: *X is*: that is to say, *X*, a perceived meaning, is declared *to be*. The situation is not represented as *X—ah!* That is merely the response to a meaning. The perception of meanings and the understanding of definitions are affairs of simple apprehension. But the judgement that a thing is possible proceeds in the medium of existence, and, as we shall see, existence conceived of not as peculiar to the human mind. An essential note, or complexus of notes, receives an existential note, and the result is not a discord. Yet some diffidence is called for in this manner of speaking, because existence is not really a separable essence from essence: it is formal-actual, not formal-ideal; an accent rather than a note.

When the parts are not mutually incompatible the possibility of the whole can then be declared. We may or may not judge them to be positively congenial, as when, taking into account the soil and the climate, an agriculturist says that potatoes should do well on a newly reclaimed fen. But for the present such a developed and realistic appreciation need not be adopted. It is enough to be hypothetical and to declare the parts not incompatible; so we are content with such examples as Eldorados and flying pigs, and more generally with the notion of object present to our mind and yet not restricted to that presence. Similarly in judging an impossibility, the reference should be to existence taken in the widest sense; we are not committed to any concrete situation, such as the case of a man named Campbell Macdonald, who was being considered as a minister for a highland congregation: 'That's no a name,' said one elder, 'but an impossibility.'

It may be urged that the note of existence we are invoking is a note in human consciousness, and that we have no conception of any other. This poser has already been put. Yet though the decisive beat is in the human mind, human truth must be keyed to another, though that is no sooner named than it is introduced to our consciousness. The reflection is not at all disturbing; on the contrary it is inevitable and what should be expected to happen from the definition of knowledge. St Thomas touches the point in answering the subtle objection that a thing is not known except as true and that truth is convertible with being as cognized, and not therefore with being as *non-mental*. In effect he replies that the saying that being cannot be understood except as being true may be taken in two ways. If it means that being is not apprehended save in that its truth appears then of course it is obvious. But if it means that being is not apprehended unless its formal truth is apprehended then it is not acceptable. Being enters into the very meaning of truth, and truth cannot be separated from it.

Intelligibility is in a parallel case, for we cannot understand being unless it be intelligible, but we can understand being without understanding its intelligibility. Being understood is being true, but in understanding we do not thereby understand truth. All this is not a play upon words. Two points may be noticed; first, that the form of truth is not separate from the form of being, for relations are not intervening entities and the relationship thing bears to mind is not really distinct from the thing itself: secondly, that the problem of knowledge is about the special act of reflexion on the possession of a real object.

41. *Possibles as Flyaways*

It would seem that if what first makes the possible possible is this association of compatible notes, even though one of them involves a reference to existence, it will be a self-sufficient object without need of factual verification, for the existence need not be actual. Moreover it would seem that the world of possible objects is opposed to what we may call the world of facts, and indeed it is not surprising that some philosophers have reserved metaphysics to the realm of purely ideal essences, which range far beyond any contingent outcropping into the surface of our experience. For this realm comprises universal and abstract types, while the world of fact is composed of particular and concrete things. Moreover the former is eternal and compact of ineluctable necessities, while the latter is temporal and precarious. The possible never begins to be possible, but always is possible. Triangularity was triangular infinitely long before there were any triangles.

Here then we are bidden to contemplate a transcendent world of eternal objects, which are neither the creatures of a reasoning logic nor the reflections of the world of experience, an order of immemorial and immutable meanings, a vision—and a snare— for a lofty contemplation that would find peace and meaning far from the bustle and capriciousness of daily life. How much richer it promises to be than the run of everyday facts, whether it be taken as a dream world or as echoing all the variations in being. For more types are there contained than will ever be realized, a greater multitude than we can ever hope to come across. Was there ever such a collection? Even the types may be particularized and individualized as we muse of all the things that might have been. Where in fact was the St Thomas of nineteenth century positivism; where the Castlereagh of the Treaty of Versailles? There it is, a world stretching out boundlessly, for admiration and wonder, if only we will go quiet inside and discover it.

Here may be found the eternal laws, older than the empires. The argument was taken up by St Augustine, but it springs from Plato. Do not think he was like Tom Tom the piper's son.

> And all the tune that he could play
> Was over the hills and far away.

Though he may not have explained how the eternal objects are mixed up in the world of experience, there was nothing evasive in his thought: Aristotle was rather his complement than his opponent. On the contrary, he argued austerely how certain were these ideal types set up in the unearthly places, how wavery and shadowy are the rest. They hold fast and true, while about us are scurrying illusions, the objects of mere sensation and opinion— 'accidental judgements, casual slaughters.'

Plato himself should not be thrust into taking sides on an issue that had not yet arisen; he should not be credited with a philosophy of escape from a scandalous world to a lucid world of intrinsically coherent objects of mind, from hearsay and guesswork to a level of lucid and self-contained evidence. Yet he set going that quest for formal beauty which may end in scorn for particular applications, which is content with an ideal meaning apart from any verification in fact, and which suits a religious philosophy which regards the world not as reality but as worldliness. It was Plato's pupil, Aristotle, with philosophy in his feet and not only in his heart, who was the intellectual hero of St Thomas when he set himself massively in his maturity to seek a physical doctrine that should not be a metaphysics in decay.

We cannot delay on the aristotelean fusion of meaning and fact at present when we are considering pure types or possible essences. It is a separate question whether or not they mingle with the facts about us; so also whether there are any facts at all. Nevertheless behind all experience there runs, like a great range of mountain peaks above the haze of the plain, these eternal and necessary meanings giving to the scene of ordinary human knowledge what stability there is. It is true that these purely ideal forms are invoked in our empirical processes, but how they enter is left unexplained. Socrates acts as the midwife for real science, which is the search for meaning, exactly defined and applied. Yet though his disciples sought to explore the real world and many were full of public spirit and sought to shape the world, the metaphysical teaching of the Academy did not encourage a real mingling of ideas with facts. A barrier had been set between humdrum experience and philosophical contemplation; the intercourse of physical and metaphysical was left problematical; and later developments of the stoic school continued the disdain of the sage for the turbulence and passion of mere incidents. The way was opened for a philosophy without pedigree and without respect for the humble decencies and human attachments, like a 'turgid and monotonous poet, with his intellectual underbreeding and inferior kind of pride, that aristocratic cad, that man without sweetheart, wife, or mistress.'

The ideas were set apart, pure forms not of this world, and the implication was seized on, particularly in the doctrines of personal salvation that flourished in the decay of the classical Greek civilization, that the world about us was neither being nor of being, but rather the pretence of being. Religious cults displaced the rationalist and scientific disciplines. The old integrity was broken. In seeking invulnerability the wise man ran the danger of frigidity, and in escaping alike from the sordidness of everyday life and the extravagance of superstitious rites, he found himself under the necessity of projecting a substitute for the flow of life. The noblest science was established in another world. Academic philosophy became, as Mr Jorrocks said of hunting, 'the image of war without the guilt and only five-and-twenty per cent. of the danger.'

As regards the problem of knowledge the way was thus prepared for treating physical nature as unassimilable by mind. This is all very well if philosophical science is to be left merely as a study of notions, but it will not do if it is supposed to be really engaged with the stuff of the world about us. Let us however remain awhile with aloof forms, and ponder over two aspects that they present, first of coherence as objects of thought, and secondly of hinting more than logical interest. From both aspects a trans-rational reality is reflected: able-to-be seems stronger than able-to-be-thought.

42. Eternal Mind

The ideal consonance of parts is the first requirement of the possible. This intelligibility is an affair of mind. There is no content without a container. In what mind is held the immutable and universal necessity? Do the ideas well up from within our own consciousness and from this fugitive snatch of reality we call ourself, a very shifty datum, or do they require that our minds are somehow illuminated from another mind, higher and antecedent? It is difficult to avoid the conclusion that their necessity is hypothetical on the existence somewhere of an external and universal mind, in whose comprehensive understanding all meanings are held.

The first condition for possibility is that an object can be thought of, and for the moment we are neglecting the supplementary condition that it can be thought of as an able to be. By the inner necessity of its coherence of notes it is thinkable apart from our contingent minds. Hence we infer a mind necessary in itself. The inner principle of possibility is intelligibility; the reference to the power of producing it is secondary and subsequent. It is because an object is intrinsically possible as an idea that it is extrinsically possible, granted the existence of a free creative power producing it in extra-mental existence, a power able to produce being as such, not merely able to transform the modes of being in material in front of him. Without as yet projecting ourselves into a non-mental field and considering the doctrine of creation, it will already be noticed that the insistence on the inner coherence of certain objects of thought carries with it the affirmation that there *is* a mind.

Whenever a necessity is discovered we are recalling what already is, a truth not just decided on once upon a time by an intelligence somewhere, an intelligence which has since turned to other matters, but a truth in a supreme intelligence that simultaneously holds all the forms of our knowledge, past, present, and to come. 'It's a poor sort of memory that only works backward,' the Queen remarked. Whenever we are so charged of the thoughts of a divine mind, our thoughts are not merely our own, but communicated from another thinker. The one divine logos, says St Thomas, contains all our separate reasons.

In addition possibles are thought of as able-to-exist. Though no straining will produce an existent from an analysis of purely mental essences, and in our dialectics the principle is true enough that from the possibility of a thing we cannot infer its existence, *a posse ad esse non valet illatio*, and that likelihood is not equivalent to fact, and though the argument, *decuit ergo fecit*, dear to some ecclesiastical writers should be treated with caution, nevertheless, at bottom, possibility cannot be entertained unless some existence is implied. There would be no *posse* without some *esse*.

A possibility is thinkable only in a mind, and this is not ultimately our mind. Furthermore in the idea there is an intention, a gesture, a reaching out to existence. A possible is what can be thought of as able to be. Every hypothetical proposition supposes a categorical, and a categorical proposition points to an *is* which no logical analysis can disperse.

We may now round back on the two aspects of essence and existence that are emerging more clearly. The possible, or what can be, should first of all be resolved into severely intellectualist elements, and not be constituted what in fact omnipotence has decided. It is curious that some of the greatest mathematical spirits in philosophy have inclined to such arbitrariness. Omnipotence at the final reckoning is the ability to make anything and everything, to produce any variation on the theme of being and to create being; the power to make what can be known, not to act according to complete caprice. Omnipotence cannot do the impossible; it does not work within nothingness; it has no dealings with contradictions.

Is the eternal mind then bound by a necessity outside itself? Must its creative power work within the limits of being? Is this the alternative to holding that there is a primary will, a free and creative appetite imposing itself as it goes along? The questions do not arise, for in fact there are no limits to being and intelligibility. Nothingness sets no bounds to being. God, if he exists, is the First and Transcendental Real. He has no destiny, and does not swear by Styx. There is no imprisonment in acting according to your nature, unless that nature is limited to a definite type of reality.

The intrinsic coherence of the ideal possible is within the amplitude of being. The first being is not the first of a series, the *primus inter pares*, the topmost and directing part of a multiple scheme. He is the total cause of everything, the complete truth of every lesser truth. Yet by a paradox that will have to be explained elsewhere he is not the only cause, and the only truth. Consequently he does not obey the law of being as though it were other than himself. A law exists first in mind. He is that mind, and he himself is the law. And as the law is necessary, so is he. It is not obedience to be true to yourself. If *per impossibile* God could make the impossible he would cease to be God. The necessity of *He Who Is* is not an imposed necessity, nor in any sense an accommodation to anything other than himself.

So we can beat back, as St Augustine did, from the necessity of meaning to the necessity of a mind holding that meaning, a mind not measured but measuring things. As St Thomas notes, the truth that is credited of things in comparison with the human mind is in a sense accidental to them, for granted that a human mind did not or could not exist, they would still be true in their essences. But the truth they have in comparison with the divine mind is inseparably communicated to them, for they could not be in any sense unless they were held in an eternal mind.

The argument is not so much from concept to thing as from example to exemplar: it is as though our thoughts have been thought beforehand. There is always this existential ring to the argument from what-is-able-to-be to what-must-be. Not everything can be possible, for if everything were merely possible there would now be nothing, not even a mind to think the possible. St Thomas uses this principle in his third proof for the existence of God, where he does not argue from a thought to a thing, but from things about us, things both able-to-be and able-not-to-be. This reflection may well introduce the next section, which considers not so much the intelligible coherence of an ideal possible but its inner expectation of real existence.

43. The Power of Existence

Possibility implies being, and being implies, not merely beingness, general reality, *ens in communi*, but also concrete and substantial being, first thing, *ens primum*, *esse subsistens*.

In saying that an essence is *an able to be* more is meant than that it is able to be an essence. That would be tautology. What is meant is that it is able to have existence. Essence is an object of knowledge, but existence engages love. These are the two sides of a single created reality: that it can be known and that it can be made. It is an essence because of the divine mind thinking it, an existent because of the divine will crowning it with reality.

In consequence some sort of distinction is implicit in the possible, a composition between its truthfulness and its desirability, roughly equivalent for the moment between its essence and existence. Essence is the intelligibility of an object to a mind such as ours, existence exclaims at a further less explicable actuality. Unless the concepts be subsumed in a knowledge of existing reality, the essence is ideal and so is the existence; the essence is not actualized, the existence is not the ultimate achievement. They are the components of a purely ideal object, the possible as coherent and the possible as being able to be more: this is the distinction between essence and existence proper to the state of possibility or ideality.

That much should be said in order to anticipate a difficulty that will be encountered in general metaphysics on the topic of the real distinction between essence and existence in existing things. Most scholastics would admit a distinction between an ideal essence and an actual existence, but this is not tantamount to the celebrated thomist distinction within existing things between real potentiality and real actuality. All we are doing for the moment is to show that within the order of ideality a duality is expressed: essences can be thought of, they can be thought of moreover as able to be. There are two accents, of intelligibility

L

and coherence on one hand, and of existence and trans-rational reality on the other.

Can we be content to contemplate an ideal world of essences? We then stay fetched up sharply before the prospect of two worlds, one above and apart from this world, the heavenly places where the mind can be at rest, the other this vale of tears, where the mind is a stranger and a wanderer. And if a stranger then also an outsider. The naked intellect might be well satisfied with the situation, happy to be relieved of the burden of existence, but there is a stubborn protest deeper within, an anguish too profound to be satisfied with a world of perfect types, a heroism that would prefer to be seedy than to remain with such nobility.

Other conclusions might also be drawn, for instance that contemplation should separate itself from the world; what we think of as events may well be left to take their course, without hope of our control, or just sufficiently controlled to allow the philosophical decencies to be protected. It would be as if christian social action were reduced to a policy of non-interference so long as people were allowed to go to church and receive the sacraments.

We should guard against excessive simplification in pointing the contrast between the ideal and the actual. If we catch ourselves attributing the dualism to Plato we should do well to remember that if he beckoned to the world of ideas he was also preoccupied with the organization of the earthly city. While he fathered a lasting tradition in religious and metaphysical philosophy, he might have been saddened to know that his political teaching was to be more successful than the Great Wall of China.

Yet even if the platonic heaven is in the intellect and the world of eternal possibles is the world of mind, this does not mean, as we have seen, that they are logical figments. They are not rational constructions in the sense of being fabricated in our reason; in contemplating them we move to something other than ourselves and our own minds. Nevertheless until we posit an actual factor, a possible as such is locked up in our mind. It has an eternity, but only on the supposition that there is an eternal mind to contemplate it; and its infinity is objectively potential only in relation to an infinite power able to produce infinitely from total nothingness and reflect on its own truth without repetition.

In other words, the existence of possibles in our mind supposes that there exists an infinitely imitable and creative being.

Anyone who would argue from the idea of the possible in his mind to a world of existents should follow the course of the third proof for the existence of God in the *Summa Theologica*. The argument may be compressed and transposed as follows:

> possible and intelligible objects imply an eternal mind;
> but there are possible and intelligible objects;
> therefore an eternal mind.

The crisis is in the minor premiss. As Burke has said: 'the majors make a pompous fight in the battle, but the victory of truth depends upon the little minor or circumstance.' It is upon the joining the ideal to the real that the legitimacy of metaphysics depends; otherwise it is no more than logic. That there are ideal epistemological objects is evident, but that they are existing and metaphysical objects is another question.

We are back again before the old impasse. How can we draw existence out of a mere idea? It cannot be done if the start is from a rational form existing in our mind, unless it be recognized as a reflection of a more total conjunction, one note in deeper assent, an open relation to a thing. We are in the position of being able to discuss possibility only because we can abstract meaning from an existent.

Nor is the transition from mental to real made by any mind. *Dum Deus calculat fit mundus*, said Leibniz; the world comes from divine algebra. But mere knowledge indeed is not enough, the creation of existence is an act of love. *Verbum est spirans amorem*, says St Augustine, the Reason breathes love; and knowledge, says St Thomas, is the cause of things when love is conjoined.

When treated as an abstraction from an abstraction of an abstraction the notion of possibility is not very productive, but if it be recognized that it draws its meaning from an assent that something is, and that able-to-be makes sense only on that supposition, then we bid fair to break out from it. The mind can begin to move from such an attitude to the inference that there is a higher and supreme mind, which does not need to treat essence as subject and existence as predicate, but whose first object, seen immediately, contains both in complete identity.

But if we accept the split between concept and thing, the transition from Descartes to Fichte is not abrupt. In the twelfth century Gilbert de la Porrée set himself the task of explaining the world by logic and then reconstructing it by the same logic, and William of Auvergne a generation later displayed the same energetic innocence. But the job simply cannot be done. The high falutin metaphysical attempt to prove the existence of the world, or to disprove it for that matter, must be adjudged to have failed. At the beginning we said that metaphysics is a humble science, or should be; it is the highest scientific activity of a mind that has left the mystery of matter but not yet probed the mystery of spirit. It is based on a historic reality. Its affirmations start, not with a soaring sweep into a world of ideas, but from a close attention to the conjunction of sensation and intelligence. *Utrum haec sit vera: homo est animal, nullo homine existente?*—can we say that man is an animal if no man existed?—this thesis was debated among thirteenth-century aristoteleans, but it was never doubted that philosophy and theology would have been unreal and pointless under the circumstances.

The physical and metaphysical sciences are not the exercising of notions; they proceed from a categoric judgement *that things are.* Metaphysics would not exist at all but for the historical event of an abstraction, and though the content released is more than what the occasion demands, this meaning remains rooted in a non-abstract subject. Abstraction has suffered in popular estimation because of the curious air of remoteness and unreality about its products: call it back and the situation is redressed. A purely spiritual intelligence would have no need to abstract, which is a function of a mind plunged into matter, committed to a material world. There it is both at home and uneasy. Abstraction should be an effort, not to escape but to appreciate the meanings there embodied and, at its best, of the meanings precisely as there embodied.

Existence is at the peak of being essence; meaning becomes fact to the ascending mind. Perhaps this is why the argument of St Anselm remains to haunt us. The morning light of mind may already catch a glimpse of past and present in the eternal present. A prophet is a historian looking forward, a good historian is a prophet looking back, and a living philosopher should be both.

So we may retreat from the lonely eminences of philosophy to take our bearings again in the common or garden world of hues and scents and song, imitating the highest philosophers at least in their respect for the lowliest forms of knowledge, and their desire for 'realer and rounder replies.' To this regard for human sensation we may add the need for the discipline and training of scholarship. Though philosophy is not a learned business we do well to distrust easy improvizations that are advanced unchecked by wide reading and experience. There is a schooling from facts, perspicaciously discovered and exactly arranged. 'The French writers,' said Dr Johnson, 'are superficial because they are not scholars, and so proceed upon the mere power of their own mind.' The critical reader may be reminded of some of the publicists of the thomist revival.

God is an artist first and an engineer afterwards. Substances are more ultimate than schemes. And so we will end by speaking not of the order of being, but of the companionship of things. We take it that there are things and different things. For I am one thing and you are another, and so also is the cedar on the lawn, the cat on the wall, the postman coming in at the gate. It will be a bad day for science and philosophy—indeed it has been a bad day—when the ordinary convictions are flouted, or even when the body and its functions are refined past all recognition. Whatever the immediate éclat, the prospects of survival will not be great. Long after a system has been forgotten, flesh-and-bones will still be asking the same questions with the same simple confidence and pathos.

There is something to be said for a high thinker who is a dirty feeder. You cannot fight human nature successfully. The reason cannot permanently frustrate the irrational drives. Accommodated to original sin—accommodated in a Pickwickian sense, for it neither condones nor is hag-ridden, but faces guilt squarely—Christianity outlives the various perfectionist cults that will continue to spring up and wither away. Similarly a philosophy that does not fly in the face of the usual human experiences will survive any system that seems to torture facts out of shape. There is no substitute for the play of imagination. Here is the meeting place of mind and matter. According to the religious philosophy of Malebranche, and he is only too typical, the senses are useful drudges for the convenience of the body but false witnesses for the life of the spirit. But this is neither good enough nor congenial to the dialectic of St Thomas.

Some illnesses are endemic. As there will always be religious systems that respond to the magical and puritan strains in human nature so there will always be philosophical systems that respond to a mental urge to violate either the reason itself or the ordinary attachments. Human truth lies in a balance: on the one side a science, and certainly a philosophical science, should always be severely reasonable; and on the other it should be rooted in the bowels of the earth. Every argument must appeal to rational evidence and yet, and this appears notably in politics, to impose a plan that does not allow for non-rational motives is bound to fail.

A time comes when analysis turns into frivolity. The great rationalist achievement of the thirteenth century lapsed into aimless disputations, and even theologians became wordy and fantastic sophists with no feeling for the *docta ignorantia* and little sense of situation; they were men who switched, in Gerson's phrase, from useful and intelligible subjects to naked logic or metaphysics or even mathematics. A time comes when wisdom is to know what are the proper questions to ask. Then may the proper answers be expected. It is a good end of epistemology to conclude that to demand a demonstration of the real existence of being is an improper question. 'Return Sicilian muse'—there is no admission here that philosophy must suffer from a peculiar weakness and a final agnosticism. The knowledge of the limits to reasoning attends every science, and particularly the empirical sciences. After many years of observation and experiment there is still no decision in the debate whether rooks do more damage to crops than they are worth, and that is a relatively easy question compared with the ordinary issues of our human lot. So with the general problem of knowledge: while human minds are confined to the processes of reasoning they will continue their attempts to escape, and they can use only those tools their prison provides.

INDEX

IMPRIMATUR:

Fr. Hilarius Carpenter, O.P.
Prior Provincialis Angliae.
die 7a Decembris, 1948.

NIHIL OBSTAT:

Georgius D. Smith, S.T.D., Ph.D.
Censor deputatus.

IMPRIMATUR:

E. Morrogh Bernard
Vic. Gen.

Westmonasterii,
die 29a Octobris, 1949